M.O.D.E.L.

M.O.D.E.L.

The Return of the Employee

MUKUL DEVA

Response
Business books from SAGE
Los Angeles ■ London ■ New Delhi ■ Singapore
www.sagepublications.com

First published in 2007 by

Response
Business books from SAGE
B1/I1, Mohan Cooperative Industrial Area
Mathura Road, New Delhi 110 044

Sage Publications Inc
2455 Teller Road
Thousand Oaks, California 91320

Sage Publications Ltd
1 Oliver's Yard, 55 City Road
London EC1Y 1SP

Sage Publications Asia-Pacific Pte Ltd
33 Pekin Street
#02-01 Far East Square
Singapore 048763

Published by Vivek Mehra for Response Books, phototypeset in 10/12 pt Aldine 401
BT by Star Compugraphics Private Limited, Delhi, and printed at Chaman
Enterprises, New Delhi.

Library of Congress Cataloging-in-Publication Data

Deva, Mukul, 1961–
    M.O.D.E.L.: the return of the employee/Mukul Deva.
        p. cm.
    1. Job satisfaction. 2. Employees—Attitudes. I. Title.
HF5549.5.J63D48   658.3'1422—dc22   2007   2007002334

ISBN: 978–0–7619–3579–7 (PB)   978–81–7829–740–8 (India–Pb)

Production Team: Anupama Purohit, Rajib Chatterjee and Santosh Rawat

This book is dedicated to my wife Manisha—
my *Kohinoor**.

* For those of you who did not know, the Kohinoor is an exquisitely beautiful,
really large and prohibitively expensive diamond.

An Infallible Road Map
to Success and Happiness

Ten simple and easy to implement steps
that will enable the hardworking person
to be happy *and* succeed.*

They will also
help the hardly working person
to be happy *and* appear to succeed.*

Conditions apply:

1. The Road Map To Success works **only** if the reader buys and reads an original copy of this book and then refuses to lend it to anyone.
2. Borrowed copies or pirated versions have been doomed to failure by *Expecto Royaltus*—a very potent and irreversible Writers and Publishers Unforgivable Curse.
3. Knowledge of the English language is imperative (unless you are reading an authorised, translated version).
4. Reading this *mantra* in poor light or in a reclining posture will reduce its potency and may give you a headache.
5. A sense of humour will greatly influence the final outcome.

Contents

Preface

Statutory Caution, Anticipatory Apology and Legal Indemnity

In accordance with the Surgeon General's warning to prevent any damage to the reader's eyes, the line spacing and font size allows for easy reading. However, the Librarian General warns that the contents of this book may be injurious to the mental health and/or sanity of the humour-challenged and/or those afflicted by an overdeveloped sense of religious (or any other kind of) zealotry and/or bigotry.

This book has no mala fide intent of any kind whatsoever. No insult or injury is intended or implied against any person, persons, organisation, community, caste, creed, religion, race, sect, sex or species. Though mostly fiction, *yet this book can have a very real impact on the quality of your life*. Any similarity to any person (human or divine), living or dead, is utterly unintentional and purely a matter of coincidence, however it could not be avoided since M.O.D.E.L. resides in all of us, in varying degrees.

While the narrative has been handled as a farce (*since reality is so boring*), the lessons inherent in the book are very real and can help in attaining the ultimate aim of all human beings—

~Be happy, not just successful

You will not be surprised to note that there is no new theory/ concept that is being expounded in this narrative; simply because the fundamentals for success and happiness (and anything else for that matter) cannot and do not change.

The simple application of basics is all that is required for most things to be done well. Essentially *that* is what this book is all about.

Most of us go around seeking mysterious *mantras* and just ignore the basics.

Most of us forget that success is a journey, not a destination and happiness is mostly a state of mind. And, of course, neither can be achieved without the perception and self-realisation of the other.

The acts and omissions described herein have been performed by people in very advanced stages of mental development, but may be attempted by you with total disregard and no great caution whatsoever, should you so desire, so long as you understand that you and *only you* are solely responsible for all/any consequences and/or damages that may/may not result.

Purchase of this book, borrowing it or stealing it from any source whatsoever indemnifies and keeps indemnified for all posterity the writer, the publisher, the editor, the printer, the cover designer, the distributor, the bookseller and all those involved in any manner whatsoever with the creation of this supreme work of art and their heirs, assigns and successors (legal and illegal), from *all and any* moral, physical, legal, civil or criminal liability of any kind whatsoever.

This legal indemnity becomes binding on anyone laying their hands on the book, even if they do not open the covers of this book and irrespective of which pages they read or don't read.

Mukul Deva

If ye can stand up, sit down.
If ye can sit down, lie down.
If ye can lie down, sleep.

Ancient military maxim (I think)

Thus,
if you can stand up—sleep

~The gospel according to M.O.D.E.L.

Acknowledgements

My grateful acknowledgements to my wife Manisha, my brother Sanjay, my brother-in-law Mukund and my friend Dhirendra. They went through the drafts endlessly, provided valuable insights and helped this book take shape.

A special *Mention in Despatches* to my favourite elder daughter Mehtab, who corrected my grammatical errors and spelling mistakes while I did her homework.

Everyday I sit by my window and watch a host of corporate warriors trudge back home at all odd/impossible hours of the evening/night. I salute all these weary souls and hope they find some measure of comfort from the pages of this book. The mere sight of them tires me and makes me thank my stars that I had the acumen and foresight to quit formal education at an early age, else I too would have been burdened with some torturously acquired qualification that would have condemned me to a high-pressure job.

I guess as the Great Bard had so succinctly put it—'*Life is but a stage and each man must play a part*.' Some of us have to work, some to criticise and some just get to sit back, watch and derive morbid satisfaction. I, for one, am content with my lot.

I would also like to acknowledge the host of managers and business owners who represented the various corporations my company has dealt with in this last decade or so that I have been operating in the corporate battlefield. Observing their antics, acts and omissions has been invaluable in helping me give shape to M.O.D.E.L.

This book would not be complete without the tremendous support and guidance that I got from Sugata Ghosh, Ritu Vajpeyi-Mohan, Anupama Purohit and Roopa Sharma at Response Books.

Chapter 1

The Book of Genesis

This is the story of Mahesh Om Duryodhana Eklavya Lakshmipati.

How he acquired such a powerful and potent name is a long and oft-heard story in this mystical, colourful land of ours. He was the only child of his parents and graced the earth with his presence only after years of prayers and penance.

"The name should begin with an 'M'," the family *pundit* (Hindu priest) announced ominously after brooding over his horoscope, "else the boy is doomed to descend to the dark side."

Mahesh (from the Holy Trinity[1]) seemed a logical name since the tiny tot displayed a marked penchant for destroying his toys.

"We must have 'Om' in his name," his grateful mother urged his equally grateful father, "for the child is definitely a gift from Him."

Thus the toddler was named Mahesh Om.

He was still in his diapers when *Duryodhana* was added on to his name, since his father was extremely impressed by the sheer machismo of this character in the television serial, *Mahabharat*.[2]

---

[1] The Hindu Holy Trinity comprises Brahma (the Creator), Vishnu (the Preserver) and Mahesh (the Destroyer).

[2] A famous Indian epic on an epic battle between Good and Evil.

A few years later his mother saw him carry his favourite chocolates to school for his favourite teacher. She was deeply impressed by his devotion towards his *guru* (teacher). This act of supreme sacrifice, beyond the call of duty, compelled her to tag on *Eklavya*[3] to his name.

Lakshmipati, the concluding addition, came about due to patriotic reasons, when an Indian bowler with that name decimated the Pakistani batting line-up in the not-so-friendly Friendship Series.

That is how he happened to have such a long and imposing name.

This poor guy, Mahesh Om Duryodhana Eklayva Lakshmipati, faced many weird and inexplicable problems on account of his name. In fact, his name exasperated not just him, but all of us. That is why soon after he entered our lives an informal committee (comprising classmates, colleagues and contemporaries) was constituted and for the sake of everyone's mental well-being he was given an appropriate, easy-to-remember acronym, M.O.D.E.L. With the passage of time Model became the *nom de guerre* under which he travelled through life.

Now, the reason I am telling you his story is because Model was a model employee. No. He had not always been one. It took him many years to evolve into one. This path to wisdom caused him to forgo six promotions, fourteen jobs, eight pay cuts, three girlfriends and one wife. And oh, lest I forget to mention, the peptic ulcers, ingrown toenails, hernia and piles that he also accumulated whilst traversing this long and winding road.

Today, however, Model is an icon of success. His colleagues regard him as a destination (not just a landmark) on the road to

---

[3] Eklavya's dedication to his *guru* was definitely platinum standard—so much so that he even cut off his thumb when he was asked to do so by his teacher.

happiness and success. His second wife is happy with the relaxed and contented man she is married to. The kids (Model and his new wife have three of them) are finely fed, comfortably clothed and have a model father who has all the time in the world for them. He lives in his own mortgage-free house, drives a decent car and wears designer labels. He holidays regularly—far more than the owner of the company he works for. His piles and hernia have been treated to extinction. The ulcers barely give off a twinge once in a rare while. Model even has a handsome stock portfolio, a temptingly high life insurance cover and a fairly decent bank balance. Finally, the icing on the cake, the EMIs[4] payable by him constitute barely 4.3184 per cent of his net income.

Today, not only is Model a model employee, but also a model husband, a model son, a model father and almost a model human being too.

This book is aimed at helping you, dear reader, to be happy and successful *without* all the anguish and heartburn that Model suffered on this road to *Nirvana* (salvation).

The methodology of becoming a model employee is almost totally risk-free. At the very best, you will become a guiding beacon to the multitudes who shall follow in your wake. At the very worst, you shall not be any worse off than you already are and people shall surely flock together and mourn at your wake.

It is pertinent to mention that there is no individual anywhere in this big, bad and beautiful world, doing any kind of work, who shall fail to find something of value to her/him in this book.

---

[4] Equated Monthly Instalment—this pleasant sounding acronym stands for the pound of flesh we pay to the loan sharks every month—in return for various luxuries that we cannot yet afford but will not wait for. In the (keeping-up-with-the-Vaswanis) environment prevalent, most young and quite a few middle-aged urban professionals fall into the clutches of eternal slavery.

It is important to highlight that Model could easily have been depicted as a woman. I did not do so only because I did not want the sexually challenged and emotionally insecure male to feel that these sure-fire recipes for a successful and happy life are only available to women, simply because of some trivial anatomical differences.

It must also be stressed that Model is not the story of any one person. It is the story of a way of life that is as timeless as life itself. On many occasions, over many years, I have observed many Models walk the corridors of many corporations and organisations the world over.

I have observed.

I have listened.

I have noted.

I have discussed.

I have pondered.

I have analysed.

I have learnt.

From all this have emerged the pearls of wisdom that lie within the pages of this book. With the grace of God, my Lord, I cast them before you.

If thee learn from thy mistakes, thou be smart

If thee learn from the mistakes of others, thou be really smart

If thee learn neither from thy mistakes nor from those of others thou art an exceptional dumb ass.

~ The gospel according to M.O.D.E.L.

Chapter 2

In the Beginning

In the beginning, Model was a keen-eyed youngster, full of life and righteous indignation. He wanted to fight against all nature of injustice. Smoking in public places, child abuse, child labour, cutting down trees, wife-beating, recycling of garbage, cruelty to animals, capital punishment, pollution, cloning, global warming, use of plastic, ozone depletion, sexual harassment, too many satellites in space, nuclear weapons, religious fundamentalism, gender discrimination, road rage and a whole load of other causes which one may or may not have heard of. In short, he was a do-gooding pain in the rear who wanted to change the world.

"Model, my dear man," one of our less tactful classmates asked him just after we all had been subjected to an inordinately loud outburst, "why do you go on and on about these things all the time?"

"All this nonsense makes my blood boil," Model retorted angrily. "I want to change things and ensure there is justice and equality everywhere."

"That's all very well Model, but why must you be so vehement and vociferous? One can bring about change without being crude and crass."

"What do *you* know about bringing about change? The only things I have ever seen you change are your clothes . . . that too, not very frequently."

"You are seriously burdened by a zealot's poverty of judgement," the other man retorted, his ears reddening with anger.

"Yeah, right!" Model snorted as he stomped off.

Much as I hate to say it about my fellow men, Model was decidedly lacking in subtlety or tact. His dress and demeanour overshadowed the highly active brain that ticked between his ears and the loving heart that beat a foot or so below. These peculiarities of his personality never allowed the real man behind the façade to be seen nor permitted Model to live up to his potential.

With that wild unhinged look in his eyes, hastily combed hair, an unruly beard with flecks of some long-forgotten meal decorating it and perpetually disheveled clothes hanging about him in strange disarray, the mere sight of Model was enough to set off all manners of alarm bells.

It is said that strong men (and women) shuddered and sought safe sanctuary when they sighted Model heading in their direction. The teaching faculty cowered apprehensively when Model stood up to clarify a doubt. His sharp wit, sharper tongue and inherent unruliness lent him the lethality of an unguided missile.

I remember the time when he was giving the on-campus recruitment interviews after we all had woman-fully (and manfully) struggled through the horrors of B-school. While walking in for an interview he tripped over the wire that one of the interviewers was using to power his laptop.

Model gave a disgusted look as he got up, dusted himself and asked, "Which idiot strung this wire right across the doorway?"

That idiot happened to be the managing director of the hiring company. Needless to say, Model didn't get that job.

Later on, when we were discussing this incident, Model asked one of us rather belligerently, "It is very easy to sit there and criticise . . . what would you have done in such a situation?"

"I'd have gotten up, apologised for tripping and said something like: 'Oh well, at least I fell down before such august company'—and left it at that," one of us counselled.

Model sniffed—derisively.

"This is not the way to win friends and influence people," she explained painstakingly. "Don't you realise Model, these people have the power to hire or not hire you."

"Who cares?" Model snorted disdainfully. "If they don't hire me it is their loss, not mine."

Well, as things turned out, they all took the loss rather bravely, I might add. In fact if Model had not been a high-scoring scholar in one of the country's top management schools with a hundred per cent placement record, I seriously doubt he would have gotten a slot anywhere at all.

If you have nothing positive to say—don't say anything.

~ The gospel according to M.O.D.E.L.

Chapter 3

Then There was a Job

Eventually, with the grace of God and some creative connivance on the part of the B-school Dean, Model joined this software company and moved to the same city where I too had gotten a job. Coincidentally, we even ended up living in the same apartment complex. We would meet almost every evening while he was on his way to the gym as I headed for the bar.

Model strongly disapproved of my dietary habits. Every so often he would drop in at the bar on his way back from the gym and sit before me, with sweat oozing from all possible pores, as he dwelled expansively on the evils of alcohol and the dangers of my depraved lifestyle.

"Don't you realise that hellfire and damnation await you unless you renounce these ungodly ways?" He would shake an ominous finger at me.

"Give it a rest, Model." I had trouble controlling my irritation.

Let me be honest with you, much as I love to fraternise with my schoolmates, I found Model was becoming an increasingly avoidable irritant. Trust me, it quite takes the joy out of an evening when you are trying to wash away the stress and fatigue of a hard day's toil with a wholesome, refreshing beer, and a hyper, profusely sweating bloke throws himself down in front of you and (after making a few disparaging and totally uncalled-for remarks about you being a lush) starts whining.

"Do you know what idiots I work with? They just don't understand me. They actually obstruct me from living up to my potential. I tell you, it is so hard to soar with the eagles when one is working with buzzards." He would moan for hours. "And my company! It drives us like slaves and pays a salary that is barely enough to feed a starving Ethiopian."

"Oh buzz off, Model. If you keep on whining like this I shall move to Ethiopia myself."

"Shame on you!" He would give me that cold, accusing look. "You call yourself a friend . . . all I need is someone to listen to me."

"That is what we all need, Model."

I did feel guilty, but please try to visualise my plight. I had to put up with this crap daily. Well, to be very honest, it may not have been daily, but it sure as hell felt like it was.

In fact, things had gotten so bad that I was almost on the verge of relocating to some remote and inaccessible colony. One day, just when I had started calling up real estate agents in the suburbs, Model walked into the bar, looking pretty upbeat and kicked with life for a change.

"Hey, pal!" He waved from across the room. "What gives?"

Rather surprised at this welcome change, I waved back at this new (and, I hoped, permanently) improved Model.

"Guess what, buddy," continued Model in his usual hyper manner, neither wanting nor waiting for a reply, "I just got promoted and have been posted to Bangalore . . . got to go . . . tomorrow." He took a peanut from the plate in front of me and threw it into his mouth with a flourish, "Isn't that cool?" A microscopic pause before the monologue resumed, "I knew you'd be happy for me, that's why I thought I'd celebrate my last supper with you." He turned to the barman. "HEY, BARMAN, MILLER TIME!" he hollered. "One coke please . . . yes, diet coke, thank you . . . and one martini for the gent here . . . dry . . . shaken, not stirred."

I was sitting there, rather shaken and quite stirred, letting the whole thing sink in. A medley of emotions muddled my mind as I tried to get a grip on what life without Model would be like. It seemed a pleasant thought to dwell on. All at once life seemed fun.

"So, they told you to move tomorrow, huh?" I said taking a sip of the martini and relishing the icy cold warmth as it trickled down my throat. "Boss got that sick of you, Model?"

"Nah!" retorted Model, but I noticed he had started like a guilty thing upon a fearful summons. Then, giving a rather weak and sheepish smile he continued, "We did have our differences and problems, but she seemed pretty sad to see me go."

Yeah! I bet! I thought to myself. From the stories I'd heard from Model about the run-ins that he used to have with his boss, I could well imagine her dancing naked on the rooftops and singing for joy at the thought of a Model-free existence. Oh well, *c'est la vie* . . . to each his own and all that.

After all, who am I to cast the first stone?

In any case, since he was soon going to be gone, I decided to let bygones be bygones and with a mental shrug reached out for another swig of the martini. It tasted even better since, for a change, Model was paying for it.

The next morning I awoke at the crack of dawn and went to drop Model off at the airport. After all, even if he was such a royal pain in the butt, he was a batch mate. One had to do the civil thing. Also, maybe, one wanted to ensure that he did not miss his early morning flight and thus have to be endured for yet another day.

"Keep in touch, comrade," said he as we bid farewell to each other at the airport. I thought his eyes had a touch of moisture in them. I was surprised and touched.

"Of course I will," I assured him solemnly.

But little did I know that it would be many monsoons before Model and I would meet again. Actually, come to think of it, even if I had known this at that time I doubt that I would have felt much anguish at the thought or realised the implications.

At that particular moment little did I realise that the next time Model and I met again it would be a very special and momentous meeting; perhaps a small step for me, but decidedly a giant leap for mankind.

Chapter 4

Now When He was in Town

Life, they say, moves on. And so it did. Time literally flew. So many small things keep happening in our own lives that it is hard to keep track of everything that happens in the lives of those we have grown up with. Thus, barring the occasional titbits of information that one got through chance encounters with mutual acquaintances at the occasional conference, exhibition or airport terminal, almost twenty years passed before life delivered Model and me to the same crossroads again.

I cannot tell you how surprised I was when I read in the papers one day that Model had taken over as the Chief Operations Officer for one of the world's largest corporations. I called his office to congratulate him.

"I'm extremely sorry sir, but he is presently away to Europe on holiday," an executive assistant with a clipped British accent informed me. "Would you like to leave a message? I will ensure he gets it at the first opportune moment."

"He's away on holiday?" I was unable to keep the surprise out of my voice. "I thought he has just joined this company."

"That is true, sir," the executive assistant replied. "He joined only last week." I felt a slight frostiness in her tone. As though she was telling me not to pry into matters that did not concern me. Taking the hint I dutifully left behind my name and number, even though I got the impression that my message would not reach Model—at the first opportune moment or otherwise.

That is why I was caught by surprise when my phone rang about four weeks later and Model accosted me at the other end.

"Hello, this is me . . . Model," he said. "Peace be with you, brother."

"*Model*!" I was unable to contain my surprise and excitement. "What a pleasant surprise?" And to be honest, it was.

"Yes, indeed it is. It has been a long time, my friend. How is life treating you?"

The mellow, measured tone caught me by surprise. Much as I tried I could not detect any trace of the old hyper Model that I remembered.

"Yes, Model, it has been an awfully long time," I replied. "How and where are you, my friend?"

"I am back, brother. I have decided to move back here so that I can be closer to my parents. They stand in the twilight of their lives now and I feel the need to spend more time with them." Coming from Model this thought startled me. I was thinking about this when Model asked, "Say, why don't we meet tonight?"

"That would be great, Model." To my surprise I realised I was really looking forward to seeing him. "Come and have dinner with us? I want you to meet the wife and kids."

"I would love to do that, my friend, but not tonight. You see, I have asked my father to join me for a glass of wine at the Guitar Club this evening . . . I picked up a bottle of the Holy Spirit while passing through Paris last week. It's a 1938 vintage, which as you are aware was an excellent year for this wine . . . so why don't you pop in a little later? We have so much catching up to do."

"That would be lovely Model, but I don't want to intrude on a father and son reunion."

"Oh, don't be silly, old chap." He was rather vehement about it. "No intrusion at all. Pater will only be with me for a short while . . . he has a prior dinner commitment later in the evening."

So it was agreed that we would meet. I put down the phone rather happy and excited. I was surprised at how much I was looking forward to meeting him after so long. I guess time does change our perspective.

Despite the fact that I was expecting a changed Model, I was really surprised when we eventually met. In fact, had it not been for the fact that we had arranged to meet, I may have had a hard time believing this was really the Model who had walked the corridors of life with us all those years ago.

That evening when I walked into the Guitar Club I saw them almost instantly. There they were, seated at a table at the far end of the bar, the father, the son and the Holy Spirit occupying a place of honour between them.

Model arose when he saw me walking towards them and hugged me profusely before he introduced me to his father. We exchanged a few pleasantries before his father excused himself and moved on to wherever it is that he was going.

After he left, Model gave me a long quizzical look. "So good to see you, my friend. How goes it with you?"

I shrugged a nonchalant shoulder (still trying to come to terms with the new, improved Model sitting gracefully before me, with peace radiating from his face and fragrant smoke from his pipe). Model turned to the waiter with a polite smile. "Some wine for the gentleman here, please."

There was a rather longish pause while the waiter poured a glass of the Holy Spirit for me. I used the pause to try and reconcile with this hugely changed Model sitting before me. His neatly jelled hair, sharp gray suit and elegant tie were a far cry from the slovenly Model of yore that I remembered.

His dress and demeanour exuded a warm confidence and an unmistakable aura of success. There was a small note pad lying on the table near his wine glass. It had some neatly written points jotted on it. A smart, state-of-the-art Dictaphone lay beside it. Model sat back, totally relaxed and content with the silence that fell upon us like a warm envelope.

Finally.

Given below is the abridged version of the conversation that ensued that eventful evening. There were, of course, several long pauses and a lot of asinine, meaningless comments in between, most of them mine, but I shall not bore you with them since they are not really relevant to the story I have to tell you. Just fill them in whenever and wherever you feel they are appropriate, dear reader.

"Model, old chap, it has been a very long time."

"Yes, it has. Much too long. Friends must keep in touch. For that's what life is all about. In the blink of an eye the sands of our time on this planet will run out . . . then all that remains will be the memories we leave behind in the hearts of our family and friends."

"Yes, of course, that is so true, but you know how life is. There is always so much happening that one simply gets swept away and loses track of things." A slight, awkward pause. Then. "I have often read about you in the papers, Model. I am glad that you have done so well in life. I'm very happy for you."

"Why, thank you so much." He gave me a polite smile. "Yes, the gods have been inordinately kind to me. Let us drink to that." He raised his goblet in a toast. "Not that you have done too badly either, my friend. I cannot tell you how proud I feel when I see your books at the bookshops and read their reviews."

I thanked him profusely. We toasted each other again.

Another long silence reigned.

Finally, when I could bear it no longer, I just blurted out.

"You have changed a lot, Model. How? Why?"

He did not answer immediately. Instead he gave me a long look, as though trying to understand why I was asking. Then he gave a deep sigh. When he finally spoke there were traces of grief in his tone.

"Yes, I have changed. I had to. Life was becoming too stressful and unbearable. If I hadn't changed I would have gone mad . . . or killed myself."

"Really? Why?"

He gave me another long, penetrating look before he answered. "Do you really want to know, brother?"

"Of course I do. Where did you put away the Model we grew up with?"

"I must warn you, it is a long and not very pleasant story. Are you sure you have the time and the inclination? Are you sure you are strong enough to handle such ghastly truths?"

By now my curiosity was well and truly aroused. "Yes, of course I am," I nodded vehemently.

There was another longish pause, as though he was marshalling his thoughts. Finally he gave an almost imperceptible nod and began to speak.

Thus spake Model . . .

Chapter 5

There was a Man Sent from God…

…That All Men through Him might Believe, and that Man was M.O.D.E.L.

"Ah, well, my son," said Model, in (what I thought at that time was) a slightly pompous manner, "Like I said, 'tis a long story. But before I get on with it, pray tell me what do we want when we are unemployed and hungry?"

"Why, Model, a job of course," I replied.

"Ah—a job! How right you are. And when you have a job? What then, my friend?"

"What then, Model? Why dost thou riddle me this and riddle me that?"

"Wait! Bear with me, brother! What then? Don't we then want a better job, or a better-paid job, or one in which we get job satisfaction, or one where we feel appreciated!"

He resumed even before I could formulate a reply.

"Isn't that true, brother? And it is logical also, since man is a progressive animal, so as soon as one need is fulfilled another emerges."

"But what is wrong with that Model? Why is it wrong for a man to want to be happy . . . or ambitious? In any case *what is the worth of a person who has no ambition*? Why should we not want to seek out things that make us happy and content?"

"Who said there is anything wrong with ambition or wanting to be happy and content?" Model retorted, but not aggressively or rudely. "But tell me old chap, how many of us realise that *it is our very quest for things that may make us contented and happy that ensures we are never content or happy.*"

"That is rather true, Model," I replied after mulling over what he had said and fortifying myself with a swig of the Holy Spirit. "But why shouldn't we all want a job where we are appreciated, which pays well and gives us satisfaction?"

"Yeah, sure! You forgot to mention that the job should not demand too much from you." Some traces of the old Model emerged as he hawked loudly: "Pshaw! A company would be able to do little else if it spent its time, money and energy on all this." Another sip of the Holy Spirit. "*This* is what I have to tell you my friend." Another (introspective kind of) pause. "Thou hast to be an exceptional dumb ass to believe that a job can be satisfying yet not demanding, pay you enough *and* have you being appreciated."

He paused to allow the import of his words to sink in. Or maybe just to have some more wine. I'm not very sure. I was busy thinking about what he had said.

"In any case, have you ever met anyone who is satisfied with the way things are? If the pay is ok, the perks suck. When both are okay then the job is either not challenging enough or too demanding? Or the atmosphere in or the commute to the company sucks. If all that is fine then the boss is a jerk or the people who report to you are shit heads who let you down with shoddy work." Model cocked a well-groomed eyebrow and gave an elaborate shrug. "I mean let's get real, boy. No matter what, there is always something missing and nobody is ever satisfied."

"What are you trying to tell me, Model? Should we not have a good boss and competent subordinates? Isn't it important that the company we work for pays us well, appreciates us and cares for us?"

"Don't be naïve, old chap. A boss is a boss. His only job is to get you to do things that you are not always willing to do. As for your subordinates, it is you who has to train them and make them competent. The company cares not two hoots how you manage either. The *raison d'être* of a company is to generate wealth—as much and as fast as possible. In today's competitive world, business has to be done at the speed of thought and a company has to ensure that money pours in from all possible windows. Then and only then can it even think of doing anything for its shareholders and employees. Everything else is just public relations bullshit. Do you really think your boss or your company gives a damn about anything except how much you are contributing to the bottom line?"

"Then isn't it vital that we smarten up and learn to manage the boss and the company to ensure they take care of us, even if they don't care for us?"

"Trying to manage your boss or your company is a mug's game, old chap. It is a shortsighted approach, since sooner or later both are likely to change. Surely it is dumb learning to manage people and things that are only a temporary part of your life. *Instead why not focus this effort on the only permanent thing in your life—YOU*. This will definitely ensure a permanent positive effect on the quality of your life?" Model gesticulated vehemently as he continued. "See, as long as you are good at your job you will deliver efficiently and cost-effectively. This will ensure that you are contributing to the company bottom line. As long as that happens, no matter what the boss thinks of you he will not dare hold you down."

"Really? Does that mean we should ignore the disgusting attitude and lack of respect they show us every so often? Should we expend no effort in being politically savvy and correct?"

"Of course you *must* ignore all this. It is totally extraneous and the results are seldom commensurate with the effort that you put in. Don't even try to play the game by their rules; you can never hope to win. Be smart, old chap, and learn to play the game by THE rules."

"This is all very confusing Model. What do you mean by saying don't play by *their* rules, play by *the* rules?"

"Before I answer that, tell me, why did you run away from the corporate world? You were always good at what you did and had been on an upward career path. Why did you quit?"

"To be honest Model, the 'S Factor' got to me."

"The S Factor?" Model queried, a bit nonplussed.

"Yeah . . . you know . . . Surplus Stress, Scarce Sleep and a Sex life as Skimpy as my Salary," I replied. "I got tired of the constant struggle . . . of perennially chasing my own tail and not even having a moment to live life, let alone enjoy it. I just couldn't take that crap any more. So one fine day I sold my Ferrari and started writing books instead. It's much easier to tell others how to live a happy life than to actually live one."

"I thought as much," Model nodded knowingly. "Don't you see where you went wrong? You tired yourself out. That is why you found your workplace so stressful. Had you learnt to play by *the* rules, you would not only have lived up to your potential, you would also have enjoyed life."

There was a slight pause as Model broke off for a sip of wine.

"*The rule, my dear chap, is not just to be good at what you do, but also appear to be good*. As long as you are good you will help the company make profits. As long as you also *appear* to be good the path up the ladder will always be clear for you."

"But how can all of us be good or even appear to be good. We are only human after all and the law of averages dictates that there will be more amongst us who are average than very good or really bad."

"The law of averages is plain bullshit, my dear man. It is just opiate for the masses. Let me tell you that most people are equally capable. Some just appear more capable than others simply because they believe they are."

There was another pregnant pause as Model partook of some more Holy Spirit.

"What we are depends almost entirely on what we *think* we are. *Most of us are more damned by a lack of faith in our ability than by any actual lack of ability*. The few who rise above self-doubt get hampered because they waste their efforts on temporary things around them instead of focusing on themselves."

By now my head was totally abuzz with confusion. I told him that.

He gave me an understanding nod as he continued. "I know exactly how you are feeling mate, for I have travelled the same road. I had to cross many crossroads of doubt to reach the well of understanding. However, the minute I reached there, everything was well. Let me explain as we go along." There was another pause as he took a sip of wine. "Success and Happiness lies in understanding and following the Ten Commandments."

"*Really*? The Ten Commandments? *The* Ten Commandments?" I asked. "The ones that Mr Moses received from atop the mountain?"

"No, no, brother," Model shook his head vehemently, "this is another set of Ten Commandments."

"*Another* set of Ten Commandments?" I asked incredulously, seriously wondering if Model had imbibed one glass too many and it was the Holy Spirit that was breaking loose. I must not lie, for a moment I was even apprehensive about the state of his mental health. I remember I threw a quick look around and was rather reassured by the brood of burly bouncers lurking near the bar.

"Yes, my friend, I have it on good authority that Moses started down the mountain with two disks. Each disk had Ten Commandments. Somewhere en route, he dropped one of the disks, causing it to crash. That was the one that had the second set of Ten Commandments on it, the ones which tell us what we must do, if we wish to succeed and live a more happy, contented and meaningful life."

"*Really!*" By now, despite my best efforts, a marked note of skepticism was evident in my tone. It did not seem to bother Model though.

"Yea, brother. It took me many moons to discover them. And let me tell you it has been a long and winding road, full of much suffering."

He gave a soft sigh.

"I often wonder how much happier life would have been for millions of human beings, if that precious disk had been protected by IBM's airbag technology and had not crashed. Or if people had been savvier and data-recovery procedures had been as sophisticated as they are today and those Ten Commandments had not been irretrievably lost. We would all have been so much happier and life would have been so much simpler. Anyway . . . *life never offers us a Restore button option. . . .*"

He sighed wistfully again. There was a faraway look in his eyes. Let me tell you, dear reader, in that brief moment, I felt myself sink into his soul. It seemed as though I was reliving those horrid years of his life. The pain, as Model had stumbled through the desert of life in his quest for the holy grail of wisdom, seared through me.

Model's next words broke in on my reverie.

"Oh well! *Que sera sera.*[1] Whatever had to happen has happened, but we must now ensure that others do not have to suffer the way I have suffered. That is why I am going to tell you this story that the Lord Himself delivered unto me when he wanted to deliver me from the evil of mediocrity and the unhappiness of an unfulfilled life. I want you to write about it."

"You want me to write about it?" I repeated like a parrot, not fully understanding what Model wanted, but no longer ridden by any doubt or skepticism. Model's demeanour had convinced me beyond all doubt.

"Yes," said Model. "You do write books, don't you? So, I want you to write a book about it and return to Mankind this timeless wisdom so that people can live happier and more successful lives."

There was a long pause, as Model pondered. And I wondered whether I was up to the task.

"Are you sure you want *me* to write about them? What makes you think they will believe me, my brother? Will they listen? Will they learn? You know mankind has never ever learnt a single lesson from history. That is why we move in circles and repeat the same mistakes our forefathers made?"

---

[1] Whatever will be, will be.

"Yes, I want you to write about them. I want you to spread the Word," answered Model. *"Just because people do not learn from history does not mean we should stop writing it.* That should not hold us back from our *karma* (duty). Today as I started talking to you I realised it is my bounden duty to return to Mankind the ancient wisdom of these commandments. I realise that God had always wanted me to do that, but I had allowed myself to get so caught up with life that I had forgotten." He leaned forward and clasped my hands in a firm handshake. "Brother, I thank you for reminding me my duty. In fact, I think *this* is the reason why God brought us together on this fateful day."

He imbibed of the Holy Spirit again and closed his eyes for a brief moment. His lips moved as though he was holding a conversation with God.

A deep, ponderous silence fell upon us. Then. Somewhere in the distance. The bells of a temple pealed. The sound arced through the hullabaloo of the city and fell upon our ears like gentle rain. My mind barely registered the sound, but Model must have heard it, for he opened his eyes, raised a solemn hand and said in a hushed tone.

"Listen . . . did you hear that? The bells toll . . . why else must the bells toll? They toll for us . . . for thee . . . for me. Yea . . . yea, I am sure. . . . There can be no other reason that we are here today. You are a writer and I have the Lord's wisdom to spread. The twain had to meet." He again closed his eyes briefly, raised his hands heavenwards and spoke in a faint yet firm whisper. "We all have our *karma*. This is mine and now yours too."

I listened to him, with awe filling up my senses and a strange tingling sensation sweeping through my body. At that moment there seemed to be a divine presence in the room. I felt the Holy Spirit flow through me as I took another swig. Then in a scarce whisper I heard myself ask.

"Model, *who art thou*? Art thou the Prophet that we all have been told shall return—to deliver us from evil and the monotony of work? In millions of workplaces, in hundreds of cities, they talk about you every day during the lunch break. They hold two-minute silences at union meetings as they mourn for thee. Each night they light candles for thee. Each morning they play hymns in thy praise. They hold *pajama* parties and barbecues every weekend in thy honour. Fervently they pray for thy return," I paused, my throat dry and my heart pounding madly with the sheer intensity of the moment. "Speak, brother, speak. *Why do you not speak*? Tell me . . . are you The One whose return we await?"

For a very long time Model sat before me sheathed in silence. His eyes closed, as though he was gazing deep into his soul. Frantic though I was for an answer, I dared not disturb him. Finally he spoke. "I do not know." Pause. "I really do not know. But I *do* believe that I am The One chosen by the Lord to be His hand in the aforesaid matter."

There was something in his demeanour and tone that struck deep into me. An inexplicable warmth flooded through me. Right there and then I knew beyond doubt that he was no false Prophet and I would profit by listening to him and learning from him. Why, I do not know. How, I do not know, but deep within the recesses of my soul, I just *knew* that he was The One and I was duty bound to deliver his wisdom to humanity. The courage of divine conviction flooded through me as I spoke.

"By God's sonties, 'twill be a hard way to hit, but I stand fast beside thee, my brother. I shall walk the path that thou showest and I shall deliver unto Mankind the words of the Lord."

Thus it came about . . .

Most of us are more damned by a lack of faith

in our ability,

than by an actual lack of ability.

~ The gospel according to M.O.D.E.L.

Chapter 6

All Things were Made by Him

Thus spake Model . . .

We are all living in a matrix. The matrix holds us down in a web of mediocrity. It traps us in a perennial stress-filled rat race that sucks out all meaning and happiness from this beautiful gift called Life.

Most of us are so busy running from pillar to post just trying to cope with the pressures of life and struggling to finish what we *must* do that we do not even think of what we *want* to do.

The few who do get around to thinking about what they *want* to do seldom find the time or energy to do it.

Most of us complete our allotted time on this planet and depart from it without leaving even a faint footprint on the sands of time.

Most of us meander through the labyrinth of life without even being aware of this.

The few who are aware of it do not know how to get past the Sentinels and break out of it. They wait helplessly for the

Oracle[1] to tell them what to do or for some valiant Neo[2] to break them out of the matrix.

Most of us do not succeed.

The few who do succeed seldom realise they have succeeded.

The rare few that do realise it, don't really know how to enjoy the fruits of this success.

Most of us confuse success for happiness.

Most of us see only what we wish to see. We fail to comprehend the real truth. *We miss the obvious as we spend a lifetime in a fruitless and never-ending quest for the devious.*

Most of us do not realise that the Oracle lies within us and that *we* have to bring out and unleash the Neo *within* us.

By seeing.

By listening.

By understanding.

By learning.

By *believing*.

Then and *only then* shall we break free.

I, too, was one of this mindless multitude.

I, too, was wandering aimlessly like a lost soul and busily chasing illusions all the time. I, too, was waiting helplessly for Morpheus or some Messiah to return and reveal the way to me. I, too, prayed long and fervently for the Lord to be my shepherd and show me The Path.

Then, one day, the Lord heard my prayers. Or, maybe, He was so deeply moved by the suffering of millions of workers on the face of the earth that he chose me to be the vessel to bring His words

---

[1] Character from the trilogy of movies called *The Matrix*.

[2] Neo is the male protagonist in *The Matrix*.

unto them. I do not know what the fact is, but I do know that one day a strange new light filled me and I began to view things differently.

That day a divine light lit up my life and I became twice blessed.

> *Success starts with self-belief.*
>
> ~ The gospel according to M.O.D.E.L.

Chapter 7

And the Light Shineth in Darkness

Thus spake Model . . .

How clearly I remember that day, my friend. That was the day I had lost my fourth job. I was clearing my desk and getting ready to leave for home, with the notice pay cheque hanging heavy in the breast pocket of my favourite black bomber jacket.

No matter how many times earlier I have carried that cross, even so it was a cruel burden. With a heavy heart, I had packed my belongings in a cardboard box and was about to leave when suddenly there was a roll of thunder and a strange, vibrant light filled the room. It seemed to glow from the half walls of my cabin—like the sheer and brilliant radiance of an LCD screen. (Maybe it was all in my head since I do not recollect anyone else hearing or noticing anything.) Then I heard this deep booming voice echo all around me. It seemed to come from within my soul. It ricocheted through me, filling up my senses.

"Model, I had told you to walk before me and be blameless. You are not treading The Path, my son."

The cardboard box slipped from my suddenly nerveless fingers and I instinctively fell to my knees. Without an iota of doubt I knew I was in the presence of The Divine.

"Is that you, God?" I asked, with trepidation and excitement evident in my quivering voice.

"Of course it is, you dimwit! Who else do you think will be talking to you through thin air?"

"Sorry, sir, but I am a bit confused since we have never met before . . . and . . . like . . . I just wanted to make sure. Which one are you, sire . . . er . . . how should I address Thee?"

"There is no god but the one God and I am The One. People have given me all sorts of names, my boy. You can pick whichever name you like."

"You mean there is only one of you, sir? Then why have you given us so many religions? They are causing huge problems on earth."

"Yeah, I know. You see, just after I unleashed humans on earth I realised I'd made a big boo-boo. You guys have caused so much death and destruction that the only way to make the planet survive a little longer is to get rid of some of you. That's why I gave you all so many religions. Religion is the human race's Lemmings Cliff, boy. It is going to keep your numbers in check and reduce pressure on the good earth."

"This is way too deep for me, sir. And I don't think I wish to pursue this conversation any further. Let us get back to what you were saying about me, dear Lord."

"Escapism, my boy. That is the bane of human beings. They *never* want to confront reality." The Lord gave a short laugh. "Anyway, getting back to you, the fact is that you are not treading The Path. The road you travel on shall give you only disappointment and pain."

"Forgive me Father, for I may have sinned. But pray tell me, how have I strayed from The Path?"

I am appalled that He should judge Mankind (in general) and me (in particular) so harshly. Righteous hurt echoes in my voice.

"I have been a loyal and faithful servant, Lord. I have given up the comforts of hearth and home and worked hard for a puny salary. I work so hard that I see my children only horizontally—when I leave in the wee hours of the morn they are asleep and when I return at the witching hour they are again asleep. I have given scarce thought to the piles that make sitting down a terrible ordeal or the hernia that makes walking a sheer torture. With legs apart and butt held high I have suffered just so that the company may prosper. Pray tell me, dear Lord, how have I strayed from The Path? What have I done Father? Pray, let Thy wisdom wash over me and absolve me of my sins. Mercy, Father, *mercy*."

By now I am sobbing helplessly. Pain and confusion rage inside me. At the same time, there is relief. I know Salvation is finally at hand, for surely my Lord will not forsake me.

"Hush child. Do not waste thy tears, for I have come to deliver thee from the temptations of mediocrity. You are feeling low today because you have been fired. But remember, failure is the *only* thing that teaches us. Failure is the tempering that we need to succeed. So hush . . . let it not get you down. . . . Instead try to understand why it happened and learn from it." There is an ocean of strength radiating from the Lord's calm voice. "To rise above yourself turn to history for *that* is where the future lies. Remember, my child that we stand where we stand not because of what lies ahead of us, but because of what lies behind us. Mankind shall never break out of the rat race till it understands this and learns to learn from history and from failure."

I felt my tears fade away as strength returned and gratitude flooded through me. "Thank you Lord. For what I am about to receive, I assure you, I am truly thankful."

I think the Lord was rather pleased with me, for there was a smile in His voice as he continued. "Son, this day I will make my covenant between you and me. I will make you exceedingly fruitful. Self-employed barons, political warlords and corporate chieftains shall come from you. Listen to me carefully and for Heaven's sake take notes, for I shall not repeat myself." The Good Lord paused while I scrambled for a scribble pad and pencil. "Therefore I say unto you, ye must stop being a loser and be born again as a Model Employee."

"Forgive me, Father, but what is a Model Employee?"

"My child, the Model Employee is one who has realised his true potential. He lives up to it by focusing his energies on the only key result area that matters—himself. Thus the results he achieves are far out of proportion to the effort expended. He seeks only to live a fruitful and happy life. He seeks neither appreciation nor job satisfaction for they be false prophets."

The world around me suddenly stopped and my pencil fell from nerveless fingers. "I beg your pardon, Father, but I do not think I heard Thee clearly, so could you please repeat Thyself? *Please*."

"I hate repeating myself," there was a marked trace of annoyance in the Lord's deep baritone, "but this time I shall, since I realise my words call for a total shift in paradigm."

"Para . . . what, sir?" I asked dimly, since I had never come across this word before.

"Oh, don't be so dim, my child and do note down my words carefully." And so I hastily scribbled down the Lord's words as He repeated them. "My child, the Model Employee is one who has realised his true potential. He lives up to it by focusing his energies on the only key result area that matters—himself. Thus the results he achieves are far out of proportion to the effort expended. He seeks only to live a fruitful and happy life. He seeks neither appreciation nor job satisfaction for they be false prophets."

I knelt by the dustbin, stunned and overwhelmed. I was repeating the Lord's words over and over again like some Sufi *mantra*.

"Stop mumbling and let us get on with it. Are you clear about what I have said so far?"

"Yes, yes, Father. I have noted down Thy words most carefully." Pause. "But, my Lord, what should I do to become a Model Employee?"

"Before I tell you that, I suggest you switch on the Dictaphone for I note that your note-taking abilities are not really noteworthy. But do keep taking notes. There is no substitute for that and with practice you shall definitely get better at it." Another brief pause. "Model, you must follow the Ten Commandments faithfully and diligently?"

"I do Father, I do. I am not a confirmed Catholic or a practising Protestant. I am not even a Christian, a Jew or a Hindu. In fact I don't have much faith in any particular religion, but I do seriously believe in Thee and I faithfully follow whatever Mr Moses told us to."

"No, no, my son. This is the second set of Ten Commandments I am talking about. Due to a hard disk crash they failed to reach humanity. I did not bother to send down a backup copy, since I have been rather busy this last millennium. In any case they are so simple I thought someone down here would be able to figure them out sooner or later and spread The Word. However, humanity has just not lived up to my expectations. Thus I have come to pass them down again."

"The second set of Commandments? Pray tell me, Lord, what are these Commandments? I assure you that I shall follow them religiously."

"No, my son, it is not going to be as easy as that. You have to travel the road and prove yourself worthy. Only then shall this timeless wisdom be revealed to you. You have to understand them because following anything blindly never helps. *You must understand that there is a difference between knowing The Path and walking it.*"

There was another slight pause. I think Boss was taking a quick sip of water. All this talking must have parched his throat.

"Of course I will give you a bit of a start by revealing to you the First Commandment rather easily."

There is another dramatic pause, pregnant with momentous implications. With pen poised over paper and Dictaphone whirring impatiently, I wait for the Lord's next words with bated breath.

"The clue to the First Commandment lies in our conversation today."

I wait for him to continue, till I realise he is done for the moment.

"Is that all? Father, can you be a bit more precise about the clue?" I cannot help the twinge of disappointment that creeps into my voice. "In fact, why can you not just tell me the first one, m'Lord, instead of sending me off on a treasure hunt?"

"Tch, tch, my son, how typically human. You want everything on a platter, don't you?" said the Lord rather reprovingly. "Sweat a little, kid and search through your notes. That's about as easy as I'm going to make it for you."

I am about to plead for a little mercy and a lot more help, but the Lord just sweeps on.

"As soon as you find the First Commandment I will put you on the Divine Learning Curve for two years and two score days. This curve shall deliver you to the shores of nine destinations. At each destination another commandment shall be revealed to you."

Another slightly longer pause. I think by now the Lord has realised that I am seriously note-taking disabled—rather I should say, note-taking challenged—since that's the politically correct term.

"Each destination shall be a new workplace . . ."

"Nine new jobs in two years and two score days! Good God! *Are you sure, Lord*? Are you sure I will be able to find nine jobs in such a short span of time? I mean it is very tough getting decent jobs these days Lord. How on earth am I going to find nine jobs one after the other?"

"By the Holy Trinity! Of course I am sure. I am God, not some half-baked placement agency. I can get you as many jobs as I want," the Lord exclaimed. "The Divine Learning Curve *must* expose you to a very diverse set of people and organisational cultures. Then only will you realise that the commandments hold good in all circumstances." I could almost feel the Lord's exasperation. "In any case you need not fret about finding jobs. As and when required you will get a call from this top-notch consulting firm located in the tall, green building beside the corn and cherry fields by your house. Just accept whatever assignment they offer you. IS THAT CLEAR!"

"Sir, yes SIR!" Detecting the mounting irritation in the Lord's tone I replied with alacrity. "Thy will be done, Boss. I understand that 'tis not my lot to reason why, but to do or die."

"Now, now! There's no need to be so melodramatic. There is no compulsion on you child. If you are not interested I can always pick the next guy on the list." There was a short pause. The Lord seemed to be mulling over something. "Come to think of it, I must tell you that I am rather surprised why the MANCOM[1]

[1] For the uninitiated, "MANCOM" stands for Management Committee. Most corporations have them and most of them are dreaded institutions the very mention of which can unman the bravest amongst us.

recommended you. I must have a word with them. I doubt if they are adhering to ISO guidelines."

"The MANCOM, Lord? You have them up there too?"

"*Of course we do!*" The Lord heaved a sigh. "'Tis such a pain! Especially that new financial controller. He is *such* a jerk that I often wonder how *he* got through the pearly gates. Oh well! I guess we all have our cross to bear."

"No point in being cross, Dear Lord, though I know exactly how you feel about it." I hesitate for a moment and then take the plunge, since I am dying of curiosity. "And say, Lord, hope you don't mind my pointing this out, but your language seems so unlike what one would expect from the Divine."

"I know what you mean kid. The thing is . . . there is so much of this generation gap banter going on that I ensure I'm always with it." The Lord snaps his fingers. "One has to move with the times you know; otherwise no one listens. One just cannot afford to get outdated. I mean, just look what happened to the dinosaurs. They were *so cool* and now they are so dead." There was a slightly longish pause as we both introspected about this. Then the Lord continued. "Oh well . . . as I was saying, at each of the nine jobs you shall be revealed one of the nine remaining commandments. As soon as you discover it, you must quit and move on. In some cases they may even fire you as soon as enough has been done to drive home the desired lesson. Got it?"

"Sure, Boss. I got that and I assure you, sir, that I shall keep a sharp eye open for all momentous and critical things that happen on the learning curve."

"Hush! You homo sapiens are such humungous saps! Why can't you listen instead of just *hearing* the words?" God gives a sharp, irritated snort. "Did I say that you should watch out for momentous and critical things? Did I?"

"No, sir. You didn't, sir. I just assumed that if it is important enough for you to want me to learn it and pass it on to Mankind then it must be something big and critical."

"*Assumed*? Don't assume, boy! Never *ever* assume anything. Check out and verify all the facts before you draw conclusions. *Always get into the minutest possible details*. If you take care of the little things the big things automatically get taken care of." There is yet another pause. "I am always in the details." I think the Lord was putting away the little devils of anger that had erupted and collecting himself. "Now, can the chatter and *listen*! At each destination I will ensure the desired lesson is driven home clearly and repetitively. This will be something that you must understand *and* follow if you want to be happy and successful." I could almost feel the Good Lord wagging his finger at me. "Now hear this and hear it well bucko—most of the time this thing will *seem* small and trivial."

"Aye, aye, sir," I murmured.

"Well, just remember that *most brilliant and important things are actually very small and simple*. In fact they are so small and simple that most of the times we simply overlook them. Even when we notice them we fail to realise their importance." The Lord paused dramatically. "These little things just don't get done, not because we don't know about them, *but because we consider them too trivial and simply lose sight of them*. Note this down my child and understand fully its import." The stress that He laid on the next few words was evident in the deliberate manner in which He continued. "*It is the small and simple things that pave the foundation for happiness and success. The results they deliver are far in excess of the little effort they require.* They are all you need to live up to your potential."

"I got that loud and clear, Lord, and I have noted it down."

"Good! And remember that none of them is less important than the others. They *all* contribute equally to creating a complete and successful you. Understand? Anyway, if I feel the need for some post-training summing up, I may drop in and rap with you again when your journey is over."

"That would be lovely, Lord. When and where should we meet again?"

"Don't worry my child, when the time comes I will find you."

I could tell He was on the verge of concluding His chat with me since His tone changed ever so slightly as He moved into the motivational mode.

"And let me tell you, Model my boy, that if you learn your lessons well and become the Model Employee I shall reward you with the ultimate gift."

"The ultimate gift! Ooohhh! What is the ultimate gift, Lord?" Excitedly. "I will Lord. I promise you I shall work really hard and be good."

"Being good is just not good enough, Model! *Not when one can be great with just a little extra effort.* THAT is what my learning curve shall reveal to you." The Lord claps his hands sharply. "And now dear boy, it is high time I made a move."

"Thank you very much Lord. I assure you I shall not let You down," I replied with humility and gratitude in my heart. "In fact I am truly thankful for Your having selected me for this important work. From this day on I shall pray to you five times every day, Lord."

"Hey! Hullo! Five times a day?" There was a distinct note of alarm in the Lord's tone. "Listen kid, I have galactic problems to deal with and a rather full Day Timer[2] so just chill it, okay? It's tough

---

[2] "Day Timer" is the registered trademark of the Day Timer Inc. They make great diaries and stuff.

enough trying to catch a wink with so many spaceships floating around the Heavens. I definitely don't want so many prayers also streaming up at me, okay? Believe me boy, my data circuits are overloaded." I distinctly heard a tired sigh. "If you should wish to pay homage to me, then do so through your actions and not mere words. Okay?"

"Whatever you say, Boss." I raised my hands submissively.

"Good, good." The Lord sounded rather relieved. "God speed then, me boy . . . *Altiora peto*,[3] *Labore et Constantia*,[4] *Hakuna Matata*[5] and all that sort of that."

"Just one moment, My Lord, I really need to know," I blurted out hastily, "Why was I short-listed to deliver this wisdom to Mankind? Is it because I am the One?"

"*You are, if you believe you are!*" The Lord replied ponderously.

"I say Lord, that's all very well but you must understand that we mere mortals are always full of doubts and need tons of clarity and direction."

"Tell me about it kid," The Lord's deep baritone had a twinkling laugh in it, "but I think you should stop beating your brains about all this and start preparing yourself for the tasks ahead."

"Preparing myself, Lord? You mean there is homework and stuff to be done? I thought you were going to give me loud and clear messages about some simple things that will help me to succeed and be happy?"

"Listen boy, *EVERYTHING* calls for planning and preparation. Just as you cannot reap a harvest without first tilling the land and planting the seed, likewise you cannot learn unless you prepare and

---

[3] Seek higher knowledge. (Motto of Auckland School, Shimla.)

[4] Labour constantly. (Motto of the La Martiniere Colleges.)

[5] No worries . . . for the rest of your days. (Courtesy the movie, *Lion King*.)

get ready to receive. The Ten Commandments are simple and easy to follow and WILL help you to succeed and be happy, but *learning is not an easy process and should never be taken for granted*."

The Lord paused, as though to give enhanced stress to what he was going to say next.

"My learning curve shall move you from your present state of *unconscious incompetence* to *conscious incompetence* and thence, finally, to *conscious competence*." The Lord's words struck home to the very recesses of my mind. "But *only* if you are ready to learn. Only if you open your mind."

There was yet another thunderous pause. Then the Lord's rich and deep baritone boomed forth with stark finality.

"*STOP BEING A LOSER, Model*! The time has come for you to break the shackles of mediocrity and learn the simple steps to the glory of greatness. Stride forth without fear. The truth is out there, Model. Seek it . . . for the truth shall set you free. . . ." The Lord's tone sharpened. "I command thee, Model! FIND AND SPREAD THE WORD!"

Then just as suddenly as it had appeared, the light receded and once again the mundane, droning hum of my soon-to-be-ex-co-workers filled the space around me.

"Lord, Lord," I whispered desperately, for there still were a lot of things I needed to ask him, "Are you there, sir?" But my words met a wall of silence. "Lord, O Lord, wherefore art Thou, Lord?" I moaned as I groveled near the dustbin. "Why hast Thou forsaken me?"

My endless pleas met a resounding silence. In fact, the only reaction to my repeated pleadings to the Lord was this soon-to-be-ex-co-worker in the neighbouring cabin, who peeped over the partition and gave me a pitying look as I knelt on the dusty floor.

"Are you all right, Model?" She made a weird clucking sound. "There, there. Don't take it so hard. It happens to the best of us. Even my grand aunt's third cousin's brother-in-law got fired once. There, there. . . ."

Her words followed me as I swept out of the office with my cardboard box gripped firmly in my hands. I cared not one whit for them. My head was held high and power surged through me.

My conversation with God ran relentlessly through my head like a never-ending stream of bytes through a lease data circuit. Even so, it took a full eighteen days of pouring over my badly made notes and listening to my feverish whisperings on the Dictaphone before I finally came upon the First Commandment.

"And, as the Good Lord had promised, the other commandments came to me, one by one, over the next two years and two score days."

There was a very long pause as Model finished speaking. I waited with bated breath, unwilling to intrude on the sanctity of the moment. Finally, unable to control my curiosity any longer, I spoke. "What are these Ten Commandments, Model?"

"No, no, my brother, not that easily, I am not going to hand them over to you like that. I am going to tell you about my journey on the Divine Learning Curve so that Mankind is able to fully comprehend the deeper meaning of these commandments and follow them completely."

I pondered over this and then nodded. "I agree with you, Model."

Thereupon Model continued, "*That* is why I want you to write down these stories and get them to Mankind. Wilt thou do that . . . for the sake of a better and happier human race?"

"Yea, Model, I will," I nodded, knowing that it was not my lot to refuse the divine. "I surely will."

"Excellent, brother." He clasped my hand and gave a warm approving smile. "So it shall be written and so it shall be done."

Hereinafter, dear reader, I shall continue the rest of this story precisely as told to me by Model. I have ensured through the painstaking use of a good Dictaphone (it's a Sony) that I bring to you in his exact words the Gospel according to Model.

What follows is the true and unabridged story of Model's arduous journey on this road less travelled and his relentless quest for the Ten Commandments that help all of us to live happier and more successful lives.

- *'Twas on this journey that Model understood that mediocrity lies more in the mind than in any actual lack of ability.*

- *'Tis here Model learnt that it is the bricks of simplicity that pave the path to success.*

- *'Twas here that Model came to realise that being good is not good enough; not when one can be great with just a little extra effort.*

- *'Tis on this journey Model realised that winners are made, not born. That greatness is achieved and not thrust upon us.*

Thus spake Model . . .

Chapter 8

For What We are About to Receive…

…May The Lord Make Us Truly Thankful

M.O.D.E.L.'s *First Commandment*

Day Eighteen P.D.A.

(Post-divine Appearance—i.e., the Day Lord Appeared before Me)

Thus spake Model . . .

By now there were bits of paper strewn all over the house. I was reading my hastily scribbled, poorly organised notes and listening to the divine conversation for about the millionth time; desperately trying to make some sense out of the Lord's words and seek out the First Commandment.

In fact, despite my new job there was little else I had done during the last eighteen days. Each and every word uttered by the Lord had become indelibly engraved on the fabric of my being. Nothing seemed to matter any more. I searched for the First Commandment as though my life depended on it. For about the hundredth time I sifted through those papers and tapes trying to make some sense out of them, but I was unable to fathom where in the confused medley of my notes lay the elusive Commandment.

"Lord . . . Dear Lord . . . I need some help here." I fell on my knees and prayed feverishly. "For the past eighteen days I have struggled and toiled. My eyes are blurring with pain. My mind is numb and awash with confusion. I have tried my best, yet I am no closer to the Truth than I had been before the Blessed Meeting."

The Lord must have been busy and my prayers fell on deaf ears since nothing concrete emerged from these prayers.

Cinderella time had long gone by and I was dead tired. I was about to push the notes and Dictaphone away for the night and stagger into bed when the mobile phone rang. I mentally cursed the people who had unleashed this devilishly intrusive technology upon Mankind. The curses intensified as I saw the calling number displayed on the evil, green screen. It was Boss. With a final curse, I finally took the call.

"Good evening, Boss. Are you also burning the midnight oil tonight?" I asked cheerily, with the clear implication, that I too was doing the same, hanging heavy in the words.

"Hey, Model, sorry to bother you at this time but I was shooting off the final proposal to the Charlie Group and I wanted to recheck the revised delivery dates. This on-demand business is just too demanding. Anyway, just go through your notes and run them by me again please."

"The revised delivery dates, Boss?" I was totally nonplussed.

"Yeah." Pause. "You don't have them?"

"I do, Boss. I'm sure I do. Just give me a moment to find them." I cradled the mobile phone between my ear and shoulder and grabbing my Day Timer riffled through its madly scribbled pages trying desperately to find the required information—since as the Lord himself had pointed out, taking notes was not something I excelled in.

Several (painful and embarrassing) moments later. Boss continues with a marked note of displeasure in his tone.

"This is why I keep telling you guys to maintain a proper diary and always note down important things."

He gave a tired sigh.

"Anyway, I also wanted to reconfirm, have you sent out those product samples to all the thirteen people?"

"Thirteen? I thought there were twelve, Boss."

"Twelve?" I could feel the irritation in his tone mounting. "There were thirteen of them. I read out the names to you. I even remember telling you to write them down so that there would be no slipups." He gave an exasperated cluck. "Which of them have you not sent the sample to?"

I mumbled incoherently and riffled through the pages of my Day Timer even more frantically. A few long moments passed before Boss spoke again. This time there was no getting away from the anger in his tone.

"I just cannot comprehend why you guys cannot take notes and get organised? Model not much intelligence is required to make a list of things that one has to do. Isn't it better to do that than to rely on your memory? Your memory can easily let you down if your mind gets preoccupied with something else that may come up.

"Boss, give me a moment please. I am sure I can remember them."

Boss made a strange (and very annoying) clucking sound.

"You want to try to *remember* them, Model. *Why?* Why would you want to clutter up your small little mind? Why not take the load off those few gray cells. It is not that tough Model, we just need to jot down such things in our diaries . . . that is why the Lord made them and the company gives them to you. Anyway, no problems, I don't think I'd like to trust your memory again. The last time you *remembered* and gave me some data you had the dates right, but you got the month wrong." He again makes that strange clucking sound. "Don't worry about it Model, I'll just check with one of the others. Maybe someone knows how to take notes and organise their work."

The sarcasm is hanging pretty heavy in the air I can tell you.

"I am sorry, Boss . . ." I begin feebly but the irritating drone of the dial tone cuts me off. I felt the familiar burning sensation in my cheeks at being made to feel like an incompetent fool.

With a vindictive glare at my Day Timer, I was about to toss it back into the sea of paper strewn all over when my eyes fell on the caption printed on the rear cover.

A Place for Everything
And Everything in Its Place.

For some reason the caption caught my eye. I knew it was trying to tell me something, but by now my mind was too befuddled to make any sense out of it. I was too tired to think about anything coherently.

It was with this niggling feeling that I put down the mobile phone and decided to call off the hunt for the night.

I was turning to hit the sack when the true meaning of the phone call and the caption on the Day Timer hit me in the eye, like a divine double punch. Maybe the Good Lord had relented and taking pity on my plight, granted me this moment of supreme clarity.

NOTES.

The thought was like a speeding bullet that slashed through me. And then I knew that I knew.

I was totally certain this was it, for had not the Lord driven Boss to make that portentous call at this devilish hour. And had not the Lord Himself laid so much stress and emphasis on taking notes. Right at the beginning of our conversation He had said, *"And take notes, for I shall not repeat myself."* He was the one who had advised me to use a Dictaphone to augment my notes. And later, towards the end, when I had asked him to help me with the First Commandment, had He not said (I scrambled through the notes for His exact words), *"You really don't have a clue about how to take notes, do you now?"*

During that whole conversation the Lord had laid so much stress and uttered the word "notes" so many times that I knew I had finally hit the right note. I was sure of it.

My scream of ecstasy echoed through the silence of the night. I am sure the Lord must have taken note of it and been pleased with me.

The neighbours certainly took note of it. I know that for a fact since one of them called the police to let them know that some- one was being murdered in Apartment F-420 and was screaming his nuts off.

An uncouth, unsavoury and unshaven policeman landed up at my doorstep just as I, steeped in my newfound wisdom, was uncorking the champagne and dancing a solitary yet joyous jig.

I gave him a hard, blank stare and asked, "What art thou that usurp'st this time of night?"

He gave me an equally blank, ghostly look and answered equally impolitely, rambling on incoherently about screams, murders and dark deeds done.

"No one is being or has been murdered here." I assured him.

"Then why were screams coming from here?"

"There were no screams," I replied. "Just one joyous yell."

He gave me another blank do-I-look-stupid-to-you look. I felt compelled to elaborate.

"Possibly whoever called you had been watching a horror movie before he/she fell asleep, which is why they were hearing things in their sleep."

"Oh . . . I see." The look of skepticism writ large on his coun- tenance clearly showed that he did not.

I tried again. Speaking slowly and reassuringly, I explained to him that God was in his heavens and all was well with the world. I was doing that when the cop threw a quick surreptitious look all around, motioned me to keep talking and with a really tiny gesture beckoned me outside the door. As I stepped forward I noted that he had pulled out a small notebook from his pocket and was scribbling something in it. A moment later he held out a note to me in a most circumspect manner.

The note read, *If there is someone holding a gun or knife on someone else inside, don't say a word, just wink at me.*

Having ensured I had read the note he pushed it away into one of his innumerable pockets and gave me a long, hard look. Despite my best efforts to return his flat, unflinching stare, I could not stop myself from blinking.

Almost as though shot in the foot, the suddenly enthused cop, came awake. Shaking himself vigorously he grabbed his walkie-talkie and called for backup. Not long thereafter an equally sleepy and unshaven flatfoot emerged from somewhere very shortly. They held a rushed hushed mini-conference a few feet away from the door. Then throwing a soothing sympathetic glance at me they mouthed in unison, "Don't worry . . ."

Both rushed into the apartment with much aplomb. Drawn pistols glistened in large hairy hands as they moved forward in a half crouch, much like a poor man's Bond.

They emerged from the recesses of the apartment a few minutes later, with bewilderment and disappointment writ large all over their faces.

"There is no one inside," Cop Two said accusingly.

"I could have told you that," I replied. "There never was anyone else inside."

Cop One. "Then why did you wink?"

"I did not. I blinked. Blinking is normal," I explained patiently. "We do it all the time."

"Oh," Cop One looked dejected. "I thought you had winked."

"No," said I. "That was a blink, not a wink."

Cop One said, "Okay. I have noted that for future reference." He paused and assiduously scribbled something in his notebook. "Next time I will not make the same mistake."

"Next time?" I asked, a bit alarmed at the prospect of having cops dropping by at all odd hours. "You mean you are planning to drop in again at such unearthly hours."

"Sir, you must appreciate this is our duty. When we get strange calls about loud screams we will have to come and check things out." The cop said to me righteously. "It is our sworn duty."

"Yeah, right," I said, struggling to keep the sarcasm out of my voice. "Now can we get on with it?"

They paused at the door, pulled out little diaries in unison and jotted down some notes.

"Do remember to lock up carefully," Cop One advised me paternally. Then, with a final wistful look, they left reluctantly.

I saw them out in total silence. I did not care one whit for these mundane neighbours or the mundane policemen with their equally mundane pistols. But I knew beyond doubt that the two policemen pausing at the door to take notes could not be anything other than a divine omen. It had to be the Lord's way of letting me know that I was on the right track.

I was ecstatic with joy and filled with the glow of divine knowledge. The First Commandment lay before me in all its pristine glory—

Thou Shalt always Take Notes and be Organised

All at once the profound depth and wisdom of this Commandment was as clear as crystal to me. I realised beyond doubt that blessed is he who takes speedy and accurate notes, for he shall surely rise.

Two decades of struggling in the workplace had not driven home this lesson to me as strongly, forcefully and clearly as those few minutes of conversation with God and my subsequent hunt for the First Commandment. I realised that I could well have saved myself a lifetime of mind-bending toil and anguish if I had been taking notes properly.

It was only hereafter that I actually started noticing the sheer impact that note-taking had on the quality of my life. It helped me to organise things (personal and professional) so well and always left me with more time than I had ever had before. I also realised how highly people thought of those who took proper and meticulous notes.

The concept of taking notes was brimming with a whole load of advantages that had hitherto gone unnoticed by me,

- You never had to feel silly when Boss called you for information that he should have had at his fingertips in the first place.
- You always had a list of things that you had to do, which you could show to Boss when he called you in to give you more things to do.
- Boss could never blame you for not doing something he had never asked you to do if he knew that you noted down everything he asked you to do.
- You could just walk out of Boss's cabin and immediately call in (the appropriate number of) subordinates and delegate the tasks to them, thus ensuring there was nothing left for you to do, except take more notes.
- Your subordinates could never deny being given a task since they knew you could track all this through your notes.

- You never had to tax the gray cells in any manner whatsoever, as long as you took detailed notes about everything.
- Even if you did nothing with the notes you took, you would always look busy and efficient while you were taking notes. This always goes down well with the Bosses when they are looking for people to promote.
- With the passage of time and practice, the handwriting got better. This is a major plus in the cyber age we live in, because everyone is so busy pecking and thumping at the keyboard that they just forget to write with their hands. (This, let me tell you, is another huge plus on the Promotions committee shortlist.)
- The wife and kids never yell at you for forgetting half the things when you got back from the market.
- The premiums for your insurance policies always got paid in time. (The mere thought of your insurance policies lapsing is enough to shatter the peace of the house into pieces. Spouses the world over always worry about this, since they definitely want to collect the moolah[1] and rest in peace when you finally go down under.)
- You were always the first in line at the bank on the due date when your deposits matured, thus maximising your Return on Investment.

I could go on and on since the list is endless. The last time I sat down and jotted the advantages the list ran into about twenty-nine pages, and that was when I was in a bit of a rush. Anyway, suffice it

---

[1] Moolah, for the truly innocent, is slang for money and must not be confused with manna (that which is sent or dropped from Heaven).

to say, the advantages of taking notes far outweighed the little time and effort it takes to make them. In fact, the only two major disadvantages that I came across about the whole concept are,

- A lot of paper and pens/pencils get used up. (This is generally not an issue since the company pays for them in any case.)
- Taking detailed notes, correctly sorting them out, arranging and cataloguing them could be a bit time-consuming. Sometimes so much of time is used up that there's little left for anything else. But this is also a short-term problem since the more notes you take the faster you get at it.

No, after due thought and consideration I decided that this was a good concept. In any case, who am I, a mere mortal, to question the wisdom of the Lord?

So enthralled was I by this whole concept that I soon became, what we in this Modern Age call, an *Assiduous Taker of the Notes*.[2] I took notes for everything happening around me. Soon it became second nature for me to take notes. (Many a time I had to make a conscious effort to stop myself from taking notes while watching a movie or making polite conversation in some social gathering.)

Whenever I have had to take a major personal or professional decision in life, I have always prepared a list of the various courses of action open to me and the pros and cons of each course.

This gives me a detailed overview of the situation, options available to me and invariably enabled me to take more judicious and balanced decisions. Also, no matter which course of action I finally resorted to, I always had a pretty fair idea of the problems that

[2] An *Assiduous Taker of the Notes* is a person who can take notes with his/her mind closed.

I would face as I travelled down that particular road. Thus I would be mentally prepared and better poised to face them as and when they came up.

"Isn't that such a tedious way of doing things?" A friend I confided in said to me. "After all even the best thought of option may eventually not turn out to be the best one."

"Very true, old chap," I said to him, not knowing from whence the words came, "only time will tell whether the course of action was right or wrong, but what is important is that we must have the satisfaction of knowing that we gave it our best shot by giving it due consideration before taking the decision. No?"

"Right." He gave me an impressed look. "May be that is why that Sun Tzu dude had written that we should seek battle only when we feel victory is possible and not just go to war hoping to win."

"True." I replied immediately, not willing to be out-Tzu-ed by anyone. "He had said that a victorious Army always seeks battle after plans indicate that victory is possible." I gave him a long look. "I can assure you that they also must have said down and considered all possible options and the pros and cons of each of them."

I returned to my note-taking and left him humming and hawing as he pondered over everything that had been said.

From this night onwards, I have ensured that my work and my life are meticulously organised. And let me tell you, my dear friend, that this has paid rich dividends and been a major factor in the success I have achieved.

That is why, all ye faithful, I say unto thee, "Forsake not The Lord and follow faithfully this First Commandment if thou should wish to walk The Path and eventually attain Nirvana."

The importance of being earnest cannot be denied, yet to succeed one has to be totally disciplined in the mind and organised in one's affairs.

Taking notes is the best way to organise your life and enhance your efficiency manifold. It requires relatively little effort and helps to translate a life muddled with diverse, unconnected tasks into a neat bulleted list.

- *The more you use your diaries to jot down all kinds of things the freer you shall be mentally and thus more relaxed and happy will be your frame of mind.*

- *They who take notes shall always be better organised.*

- *Better-organised people are better poised to seize opportunities that enable them to succeed.*

- *Better-organised people have more time to enjoy life and the fruits of their success.*

- *The meek may or may not, but the better-organised people shall definitely inherit the earth.*

Thus spake Model . . .

M.O.D.E.L.'s *Second Commandment*

Month One and Day Nineteen P.D.A.

Thus spake Model . . .

Having basked in the glory of finding the First Commandment and mulled over it for a few days to make sure I had understood all possible nuances to it, I sent up a fervent prayer to the Lord to let Him know that I had completed the first allotted task. Barely a few hours later a lady from the Lord's consulting firm called me.

"You have been most highly recommended to us," she said in a pleasant, but very professional tone, after we had been through the mundane formalities of introducing ourselves. "So if you have the inclination we have the job."

"Of course I have the inclination," I assured her. "Just point me in the right direction, dear lady."

I carefully noted down the address of the company and the details of the person I had to report to. My morale was high and eagerness champed at my soul.

"And listen, dress up really smartly when you go there," she added. "The company has got top rank in the Best Dressed Companies survey for this year".

I assured her I would and then rung off.

The company chosen by the Lord where I was to uncover the wisdom of the Second Commandment was The AW-SWISH Blade

Company. It was a highly focused, aggressive company and the undisputed market leader in cutthroat razors. Its latest innovation—the double-sided cutthroat razor—had stormed the market and made mincemeat of the competition.

These days you could not go anywhere or turn a page in any newspaper or magazine and not have the latest advertisements hit you in the eye. They went:

AW-SWISH CUTTHROATS
Nothing else will do.

And the other one screamed,

AW-SWISH DOUBLE-SIDED CUTTHROATS
Everything else is just a razor.

"AW-SWISH is supposed to be a hellish place to work in," a friend I ran into at the club told me that evening. "The survival rate at AW-SWISH is shockingly low since the wages and benefits are rather poor and the work is said to be killingly hard."

"Oh well," I replied, not very happy with this information, but undaunted nevertheless. "Whatever will be, will be. How tough can it be? In any case there can be no gain without pain, my friend."

I could not let anything deter me one whit. In fact, it gladdened my heart to get their appointment letter barely an hour after my interview with their Director, Human Resources (HR). I was just dying to get started and complete the nine tasks that had been assigned to me.

Not that they could have turned me down since I was the chosen one and the Lord was in my corner rooting for me. But I also choose to believe that he (the Director HR) had been highly impressed

with the assiduous manner in which I had taken extensive notes
during the interview and the fact that I had taken great care to dress
up really sharply, as though I was responding to a royal summons
from Caesar himself. I was also rather thrilled to note that even he
(the Director HR) had taken pains to dress up well for the meeting
and was looking really sharp despite having the misfortune of starting
life with a major handicap in the looks department.

For my first day on the job I arrived at the office all spruced up
to the nines since I wanted to make sure I made *the* right impact
on everyone. Also, because the rumours thronging the marketplace
were that the Boss was a real stickler when it came to dress code and
conduct. According to grapevine gossip her favourite statement was,
"First impressions are the ones that count and you get only one
chance to make that impression." She generally rounded it off by
declaring, "Appearances maketh the man, or woman, as the case
may be."

I think the grapevine gossip must have gotten the facts straight
this time since I found all my co-workers really smartly dressed.
I also saw a plethora of stickers and banners all over the place.
They boldly proclaimed things like, *a dirty collar gets you a holler*; *a
loose tie gets you a black eye*; *a shoe without polish is like salad without
garnish*; and *long unruly hair is as bad as polluted air*.

I got the distinct feeling that someone up the ladder was ensuring that even the dimmest wit got the message that dressing up right
was important.

I had barely reached the really tiny cubicle that had been allotted to me and was settling my stuff down when someone from the
neighbouring cubicle called out to me in an urgent whisper.

"Hey! You! The new guy in the pin-striped suit with a double
crease on the right trouser leg. Shake a leg and move it. On the
double, pal. There's a Disciplinary Committee meeting in Prinz-
Albrecht-Str-8."

"The Prinz-Albrecht-Str-8? The Gestapo Headquarters?"

"No, our Central Conference Room. Wait till you see it, then you will know why we call it that?" The man laughed grimly. "Anyway, there is no time for chatter. Come quickly, the Boss is on her way. We must reach before her."

I hurried along behind him thoroughly confused and puzzled. There was quite a large crowd gathered in the Central Conference Room when we reached there. Even now more people were rushing in from all points of the compass. Despite the flurry of movement a strange silence engulfed the room. I was mulling over this when the Boss entered.

Dressed to kill in that chic, smart business suit, she strode in regally and walked up to the battleship-gray podium. Her stiletto heels beat a deadly tattoo on the highly polished wooden floor.

For quite some time Boss didn't say a word. She just stood before us with a mobile phone in her hand and kept clicking the lid of the phone open and shut as she glared at us. There was something seriously sinister about the mechanical clicking sound that emerged from the phone as the lid slammed shut repeatedly. It reminded me of the snick of a rifle being cocked. Finally she looked at one of us in the gathered multitude and spoke.

"Lamech!" The word crackled out like a shot.

Ominous pause.

"Why?"

There was a longer, even more ominous, pause.

"Art thou not aware of Company Policy?"

A fevered hush ran through the gathered multitude as Boss invoked the ultimate corporate deity—Company Policy.

The crowd parted instinctively to reveal Lamech from amongst us. All at once he stood alone and isolated. (Lamech, I learnt later, was the VP, Institutional Sales. It was his job to sell AW-SWISH cutthroats to the Barbers and Hairdressers Associations all over the land.) Lamech didn't say a word. He just looked at her with a wild, terrified look in his eyes, with the distinct shadow of stubbly undergrowth staining his chin.

Boss gave him a long, unflinching stare. Finally, she clapped her hands thrice and all at once, as though by magic, I saw three tall, gaunt women in black emerge from one flank of the crowd. (I learnt later that they were the VP Admin, VP HR and VP Staff Welfare). All three appeared to be rubbing their hands in glee. The knife-edged creases of their midnight black suits stood out so sharply that they seemed to cut ominously through the air like a hot knife through butter. Their very appearance was enough to suck all happiness out of a person.

Boss gestured imperviously towards Lamech and, dementor-like, they converged upon him and literally began to drag him down the hallway towards Lubyanka Square, the dark and dank bowels of the building where the parking lot was located.

Sheer panic was writ large on his face and he began to sob and yell wildly. "Mercy! For the Lord's sake! Mercy!"

"Who's Mercy?" Boss turned towards the rest of us gathered there watching over the whole proceedings with fear and morbid curiosity crowding our hearts. From amongst us emerged a small, scared-looking damsel.

"*You* are Mercy?" Boss gave her an amazed look. "Why art thou looking so strained? And what is that ink spot doing on your shirt pocket?" Then, shrugging as though the answer was not really of consequence, she pointed at Lamech, "Dost thou know this man?"

"I don't, Boss, I don't. And the ink spot just happened a moment back when my pen leaked . . . I am sorry, Boss . . ." Mercy pleaded wildly with folded hands. The tears that fell from her eyes swept forth like a flash flood washing away her mascara and eye shadow.

"I swear I don't know him, Boss. I am chaste. I have just noticed him once or twice during lunch."

Boss gave her a long, hard look and then clapping her hands decisively, gestured towards her. In a thrice the Managers Admin, HR and Staff Welfare converged on her and she too was literally carried off kicking and screaming towards Lubyanka. Then we all, with bated breath and in fearful silence, waited.

It was not a very long wait. A scant six minutes had elapsed when the elevator doors hissed open and vomited out the six dreadnoughts, the VPs first and then the Managers. They came up and stood deferentially before Boss, who was still toying menacingly with the mobile phone in her hands.

Boss: "Have you ensured they are gone?"

The VPs chanted out in unison. "Yes, Boss, we ensured they drove past the security barriers. With these very eyes we watched them go."

Boss: "Have you withdrawn their Lubyanka car-parking stickers and access control cards?"

The VPs: "Yes, Boss! Here they are." And the VP Admin held them up high in the air for all of us to see.

Boss: "Have their names been erased from the access control systems?"

VP Security: "Yes, Boss. They have been erased."

Boss: Turning to the rest of us gathered there. "Let this be a lesson to all of you. *Only the confident and the well dressed shall inherit the earth*. Those of you who fail to live up to the Smart Dress Code of the company shall meet the shabby fate they deserve." She shut the lid of the mobile phone in her hands with one final, decisive click and turning on her sparkling stiletto heels fired a parting shot as she left. "Those of you who do not obey Company Policy shall definitely be erased."

There was total silence for a very long time after she left. Nobody moved. The silence was broken when the VP Admin turned to the other two VPs with an evil half smile on her face. "When shall we three meet again?"

Security: "When there's hurly-burly to be done."

Staff Welfare: "Say, why don't we get together at the Blasted Heath (that, I learnt later, was what the company cafeteria was called) for a spot of lunch? All this work makes me hungry." The other two nodded vigorously and the three VPs moved off with their Managers in tow.

Shortly thereafter all of us also dispersed. The rest of the day passed by in a heavy, uncanny and uneasy silence.

"What hath Lamech done?" I asked one of my older colleagues in a hushed whisper when we were walking out of the office that evening.

He threw a quick glance all around and then replied in an equally hushed whisper. "The fool was quite good at his job, but he used to move around without shaving for days, even though Boss has issued very clear instructions that all AW-SWISH employees, regardless of sex, must always appear in public with no hair on any part of their bodies except the head and eyebrows. The idiot just refused to listen to anyone and went about sporting foliage. Oh, well . . ." he shrugged, "the diktat is clear—we must give a loud and clear message to the ignorant, sweaty and unshaven masses about the need and efficiency of our products. In any case paragraph 17(d), sub-section 11.3 of rule 4 clearly states that appearances are of supreme importance and there will be no compromise on this account."

The long, penetrating look he gave me caused my chin to itch guiltily and made my hair stand end on end.

"You are new around here, so let me advise you to read the Rules of Engagement thoroughly and follow them blindly. Otherwise things can get quite hairy around here."

Me. Lamely, "But why was Mercy fired? What had she done? I didn't see her with a beard or moustache?"

He. Giving me a hard *are-you-trying-to-be-funny* kind of look. "Let's not split hairs about this, my friend. Have you heard of guilt by association? Did you see the shoddy manner in which she was dressed?"

Then he threw a quick look over his shoulder at the slight double crease in the lower half of the right leg of my trouser, shuddered and hurried away from me.

The next day the headhunting company sent some more lambs for interview and by nightfall two new, smartly dressed and clean-shaven people joined us in place of Lamech and Mercy. Thus the circle of life continued.

Divine placement or not, I decided that prudence was definitely the better part of valour and spent the next few days and nights reading and memorising the Rules of Engagement. I was petrified about what the Lord would say and do if I messed up the very first job itself. In any case, there is such a thing as basic pride and self-respect. I definitely didn't want to look like a fool when everyone around me was so spruced up and looking sharp all the time.

A week later I had just entered office and was getting ready to start the day's toil when my phone rang. "Boss wants to see you at once," the crisp voice of Boss's executive assistant informed me. "Now!"

"Me? Why? What have I done?"

"She interviews all newcomers on the Seventh Day."

"I am on my way," I replied in equally crisp tones.

Frantic with anxiety I rushed to the washroom to reconfirm that there was no hint of hair growth on any part of my face or any unwanted crease on any part of my suit. Then I straightened my tie and ran a quick brush of polish over the shoes. This done I ran to her office and stood before the executive assistant who picked up the intercom to let Boss know that I had arrived.

"Sit!" said the fair and lovely secretary draped in a starched sari. "The Boss will see you shortly."

I sat there, running over the Rules of Engagement in my anxiety-ridden head in an endless litany. I also ran over each and every action of mine to see if I had erred anywhere. I hadn't. I couldn't have, because the only thing I had been doing the whole week was reading the Rules of Engagement. Even so, by the time she called me in my mental health had suffered and deteriorated considerably.

"Waiting is ten times worse than the frenzy and bloodletting of actual battle." Some buddies of mine who are in the army had often told me. Well that day I found out how right they are.

By the time I was called in I had begun to sweat profusely and my blood pressure was decidedly quite a few notches higher. An unfamiliar nauseating feeling was surging through my stomach and making me want to retch. With all my will power I resisted the impulse since I did not want to spoil my clothes and go in looking like a wretch.

I was almost about to lose control when I saw the Boss's secretary pick up the intercom. Then she looked up at me and called out loudly, "NEXT!"

I jumped up guiltily and almost ran up to Boss's door. Knocking at the cabin door I entered at her commanding "come in."

Boss was sitting erect and assiduously removing a microscopic piece of lint from her coat when I entered. On the wall immediately behind here was this huge computer generated banner.

Arbeit Macht Frei

Just to ensure that even the German-challenged were able to get the drift loudly and clearly, Boss had placed the English language translation below it.

Work Sets You Free

For some reason the words seemed very familiar. I knew I had seen them before. Then I remembered. I had seen them on the arched metal grill above the main gates of the erstwhile concentration camp at Auschwitz.

"Welcome to AW-SWISH!" Boss arose from her chair and extending her hand shook mine firmly. I noticed Boss run a detailed, lingering look over me—from the tips of my hair to the toes of my shoes. The roots of my hair tingled in anticipatory apprehension, but whatever she saw seemed to have met with her approval, for there was a hint of a smile in her eyes as she motioned me to sit down.

Knowing that I had passed a crucial initial test I heaved a mental sigh of relief as I sat down. The little extra effort I had been taking on dressing up seemed to have paid rich dividends since it had made a positive impact on the way Boss perceived me.

Then, even before my butt had touched the stiffly starched seat cushions, she spoke in a low hoarse whisper. "Say! Listen! Let me make you an offer you can't refuse."

"Yes, Godmother. I am yours to command," I said softly, matching her tone.

Boss's tone immediately sharpened and climbed a few octaves. "Speak up I say. I hate people who mumble! And for heaven's sake look me in the eye when you talk to me."

Involuntarily stiffening my spine and drawing erect, I looked her straight in her eyes and shot back in a much louder tone. "Ma'am, yes, ma'am!"

Boss relaxed a mite in her chair as though momentarily appeased by my response.

"Good. Much better. Do you see . . . when you speak clearly and look the other person in the eye as you talk, you will normally encounter the same forthrightness from the one you are communicating with."

I nodded and was about to speak, but Boss continued unchecked.

"Now listen, we have three golden rules here. I am sure you have heard them before in this week that you have been here but I just wanted to repeat them to ensure there is not even an iota of ambiguity as regards our vision and our mission."

She paused. I didn't say a word. I don't think she wanted me to in any case.

"The first is right there," she waved her hand at the banner behind her. "Make sure you never forget it."

"Yes, Boss. I got that. I will work really hard."

"Really! And you think that will set you free?"

"Of course, Boss. The harder I work the more I will earn and the sooner I can retire and relax," I replied eagerly.

"What a gas," Boss gave a short, snappy laugh. "You should not believe everything you read Model. That," she again pointed at the poster, "is one of the biggest jokes that has been played on millions." She gave me a long look, as though daring me to contradict her. I refused to take the bait. "Boy! The only way you shall ever be free is if you work smart . . . not just hard."

"Yes, Boss," I nodded after a moment's thought. "I get what you mean."

"Good!" She nodded approvingly. "The second rule is that you must always dress in strict compliance of the Rules of Engagement. Dressing well is very important. That's the first thing people notice about us and that is what they use to make their first impressions about us."

She wagged a solemn finger at me.

"Remember, Model, first impressions are the ones that last. Dressing smart is the first and most basic sign of success. That is why at AW-SWISH we lay a lot of stress on dress and enforce the Rules of Engagement brutally. Nobody around here forgets them. The second they do, they are not around here any more."

This last one was from the side of her mouth.

"See?" There was a bone-chilling menace in her stony eyes. Slivers of cold fear slithered through me. "It's not healthy to forget the Rules."

I replied in my most sincere and reassuring tone. "Yes, Boss. I know them by heart and I will follow them blindly with my body and soul."

I doubt Boss heard what I had said. She continued in short staccato sentences: "Don't think. Do what I tell you."

"Do what, Boss?"

"Hist! Dumkopf! That is the third rule. Got it? Don't think. Do what I tell you."

"Yes, Godmother."

Boss gave me a long, hard look. "Remember these rules, sonny. If you want to stay healthy and wise, remember them *and follow them*. We are in the cutthroat business and we have to bond with the best. We don't accept anyone who strays from the Rules of Engagement. To dress badly and appear untidy is to disobey. To disobey is to sleep with the fishes. Okay?"

"Yes, Godmother. I can assure thee I will do all that thou shall command me. I shall always dress well and help thy rule flourish and the company prosper. I hope that whoever rebels against Thy orders and disobeys Thy words shall be terminated."

"Yes! Always remember," said she enthusiastically and energetically, from the corner of her mouth, pumping her right hand in the air. "I am the law!"

I leapt up to my feet and hailed loudly. "Hallelujah!"

"Good! That is the spirit." I could see she was pleased and I knew I was on the right track. I felt my stock with her rise as I resumed my seat. She mellowed a bit and with a faint flicker of a smile pointed at the coffee and cookies kept on the table. "Try some . . . they are lovely."

They looked lovely and emitted a decidedly delicious aroma.

"Thank you, Boss, but I am on a diet," I politely declined. Her broad approving smile warmed the cockles of my heart.

Shortly thereafter I took leave of her and left. She saw me off with another faint smile and an almost gentle, "Out, out damned spot".

As I reached the cabin door and turned to bid her farewell she gave me an energetic thumbs up and bellowed enthusiastically, "Remember, you are an AW-SWISH legionary now . . . as such you are already dead . . . so go forth without fear."

Her words sent an involuntary surge of adrenalin pumping through my blood. I could not control myself from a final salutation and bellowed back equally enthusiastically, "We, who are about to work smart and not just hard, salute you . . . MA' AM."

Then I left her cabin as rapidly and gladly as the Israelites fleeing from the Egyptians after four hundred and thirty years of oppression; enthused I was, but not stupid to linger in the presence of Boss for even a second longer than mandatory. Very early in life I had learnt never to stand for too long in the front of the Boss's front or the donkey's rear. One can never be sure when the former may suffer a mood swing and bite your head off or give you some more work, or the latter may decide to kick or fart. Neither of these possibilities holds any kind of appeal to me. I had learnt to get going when the going was good.

A few days later, I was discussing this whole issue about AW-SWISH and its huge focus on dress and appearances with one of my pals who had popped in for dinner. He is a senior, highly experienced and much decorated officer in the administrative branch of the Royal Air Force.

"Of course, Model!" He said to me. "That is so true. Even in the Royal Air Force Admin our motto is to always dress sharp and exude a positive attitude by saying yes to anyone who asks for anything."

"Brother, I agree that dressing sharp is important, but how do you ensure that you are able to do whatever anyone wants? It is impossible to please everyone."

"My dear boy, appearances are *everything*. The way we dress and carry ourselves is the way others will treat us. Life in uniform has taught me one simple truth—*if you are dressed smart and are present at the right place at the right time most of the battle is already won*."

He paused for a refreshing swig of beer.

"As for pleasing everyone, we don't even try to do that. But we never ever say no to anyone. We Royal Air Force types are trained to be totally positive in our thoughts and words. The deeds are dictated by ground reality. Only the Boss's will gets done. As for the others, if it is possible and convenient we do it, if it is not we don't even talk about it. But in no case do we ever say no to anyone. Saying no is a big no-no and reflects poorly on one's leadership skills. It is simply not the done thing to do. Not cricket, old chap."

He took another large swig of beer.

"Dressing up right and having a positive attitude, that's what success is all about."

He then thumped down the beer mug decisively as though indicating that this conversation was over and there was no need to repeat the obvious.

I thought over his words that night and also mulled over everything that I had seen at AW-SWISH and I realised how logical it all was.

Ultimately, actions didn't count for much. It is the way we dress, the way we carry ourselves and the positive attitude we display that matters.

This was reinforced by a series of events during the days that I spent at AW-SWISH. Many were the lost souls who forgot the words of the Lord and did not adhere to the Rules of Engagement. They fell by the wayside like autumn leaves and vanished without a trace like marines in Iraq. Bleak were the things that were muttered about the fates that befell them. Dark rumours flowed hither and thither and drove shivers down the spines of strong men and women.

As the Good Lord had promised, repeatedly this point about dress and appearance was driven home to me and I knew without doubt that the Second Commandment just had to be—

Thou Shalt Always Dress Smartly and Exude a Positive Attitude

Just to make doubly sure that this indeed was the wisdom that the Lord wanted me to absorb from AW-SWISH, the very next day I wore slip-ons to work, even though the Rules of Engagement were clear that when wearing a tie the employee must wear shoes with laces, for that is what Emily (of the Post fame) says is the thing to do. I was terminated, without even a reference.

This confirmed to me that I had indeed discovered the ancient wisdom of the Second Commandment. Otherwise there was no way in hell they could have fired me, since I was a divine placement and could only leave AW-SWISH once I had completed the assigned task.

I knew that the Lord's objective from this destination on the learning curve had been completed and I happily moved on having learnt my lesson on dress, appearance and attitude.

Thereafter I have never appeared in public unless I am smartly dressed, with my shoes sparkling, my chin as smooth as a baby's bottom and a positive attitude literally oozing out of all possible pores.

And let me tell you, my friend, this has contributed to my success far in excess of the little effort I have taken on my appearance. Not only that, it has also ensured that I am always looking good, feeling good and confident about myself.

- *People who dress smartly make a good first impression.*

- *First impressions are the ones that last.*

- *People will treat you the way you treat yourself. They tend to reflect the attitude they encounter.*

- *Successful people always display a positive attitude, since a positive attitude begets a positive response.*

- *Smart dress and a positive attitude make you feel good about yourself and enhance your self-confidence, thus augmenting the success one attains.*

- *A positive attitude not only augments your success, it also helps you to be happy and enjoy the fruits of your success.*

- *To succeed one must "think" and "look" successful.*

Thus spake Model . . .

Month Four and Day Sixteen P.D.A.

Thus spake Model . . .

After having my name erased from the access-control systems and being bounced out of AW-SWISH not too ceremoniously, on my way home I made a quick stop at the bank to deposit the final settlement cheque they had thrust into my hands as I was escorted across the final barrier. I had barely entered the house when the phone rang. It was the lady from the Lord's consulting firm.

"What happened at AW-SWISH?" She asked without any preamble.

"I'm not too sure . . . apparently my dress sense was not up to the mark," I replied, knowing that I could not tell her of my divine quest. "I guess I wasn't swish enough for them."

"Oh well . . . whatever," She said dubiously. "This was most unfortunate . . . you need to pay more attention to the way you dress and carry yourself if you ever want to amount to anything," she clucked authoritatively. "Anyway, our Managing Director wants me to offer you another position . . . if you are interested."

"Of course I am interested," I said heartily. "But I will only be able to go for the interview on Monday." I was rather glad that the Lord was keeping such a sharp eye on my progress, but seeing that it was Thursday I decided to take the weekend off for rest and recuperation. (Let me tell you, my friend, toiling for the Lord is tiring work.)

"Really! Why? What's wrong with tomorrow?"

"I'm tired . . . I need some time to unwind."

The headhunting lady was not at all bucked when she heard this, but seeing that I was adamant finally relented. Giving me the coordinates (date, time, place, person, company and address) she gave a loud sniff and hung up, more than a trifle miffed.

The coming Monday, I was happy to find that the Lord's learning curve had delivered me from the vicious, cutthroat competition of the AW-SWISH Blade Company to the calmer and greener pastures of WATCH YOUR BACK SECURITIES—*We Make Your Money Work*. (That's what the baseline of the company logo said. It never said whom they made the money work for.)

WATCH YOUR BACK was a really calm place to work in. They went out of the way to promote a serious and serene atmosphere, much like a blue-blooded bank. Everyone had to wear snowy white shirts and gray pin-striped suits and talk in calm, measured tones.

It was also definitely green not only because it dealt with money, but also because every possible inch of office terra firma was covered with grass, trees, potted plants and stuff like that.

"Boss started doing this ever since he got back from Las Vegas," a co-worker at WATCH YOUR BACK explained. "Because green things release oxygen into the atmosphere the whole day."

"Why . . . what's the connection?" I asked nonplussed.

"Apparently he was attempting research with numeric combinations at a casino when he learnt that the casino authorities periodically pump oxygen onto the floor to make sure the gamblers are always charged with energy and don't feel sleepy. I guess Boss also wants everyone fully charged up and not falling asleep."

I have no clue whether this is true or not but I thought it all rather weird. I told my co-worker that.

"Oh well, but then that's Mr Mike M. Ilken our CEO, for you. Though a brilliant man, he has a penchant for such theories." He waved an arm around at the office. "Just look at his concept of watching your backs. He has had the office designed in such a fashion that each one of us has our immediate supervisor watching our back all the time."

I looked around with more interest this time and saw that this was indeed true. The (few) gaps in the relentless surveillance were more than adequately covered by close circuit television cameras, voice-activated bugs, access control devices and recording of all telephone calls. I am pretty certain that George Orwell must have had the Boss in mind when he wrote "Big Brother is always watching."

In fact, the CIA, the KGB and the Mossad could easily have taken some tips from him. I'm not kidding. This same worker who had been giving me all this inside gen vanished without a trace a few hours hence. But that was to come a bit later.

"He is a bit of a weirdo," the same helpful co-worker continued. I guess he was trying to help me settle down hence was putting me up to speed on the local gossip. "Do you know about his hiring policy?"

"No, I can't say that I do," I replied.

"Well, Boss is of the firm opinion that you are fit to be a card-carrying member of WATCH YOUR BACK only if you are single and plan to remain so."

"Really?"

"You see, Boss is convinced that no one can be happily married and happily working at the same time since both are full-time commitments. He feels it is physically and mentally impossible for anyone to meet the directly conflicting requirements of a job and a marriage," the co-worker told me. "Boss is clear that to do anything well one has to be fully focused on it."

I nodded gravely and pondered over it well into the night. It seemed logical.

Of course, I soon learnt that this hiring policy was not written down or ever discussed. I guess Boss was smart enough to know that one has to watch one's back against these weird people who go on and on about discrimination and all.

In fact WATCH YOUR BACK took great pride in being an equal opportunity employer, but with the ever so slight (unspoken) nuance that it extended these equal opportunities only to those who were smart enough to stay away from marital bliss and other such dubious distractions.

The sum of all these fears was that one never got to hear of a WATCH YOUR BACK employee who had to take maternity or paternity leave, attend a PTA meet, rush home because the kid or the wife was ill, or seek a loan because the school fees had to be paid.

To be honest, by and large the rank and file at WATCH YOUR BACK was a happy lot. Though, of course, there were a few amongst us who roamed about with that harried look that made us all suspect that they were much married and lying through their teeth about it.

I remember once we were having an open house in the garden outside the main office block. Suddenly, this middle-aged bloke named Krishna Guha Bhattacharya whom we all affectionately called KGB, a senior supervisor in the Vigilance Department, got up, looked heavenwards and said, "I need to go, my daughter . . . I mean, my dotty nephew's flight has landed . . . I must go to pick her up."

"Her? Him, you mean," one of us asked as we all gave him suspicious stares. "How do you know? Did you see the plane go past? Is that why you were staring up at the sky?"

"Yes, yes, I mean him. I must go and pick him up. No, of course I didn't see the plane go by. I just got a text message on my mobile phone," he replied, a mite flustered. Then, seeing the plethora of sceptical and accusing looks being thrown at him, he added, "My nephew cross-dresses a lot, that's why we sometimes refer to him as her."

"Ah, so!" The inquisitor amongst us replied with a sigh of relief. Most of the accusing looks were replaced by nods of understanding.

KGB, cocking his ears at the sky, abruptly said, "It's going to rain. I think I must go now." Saying so, he rushed off.

Anyway, let me get back to the main story.

One day Mr Mike M. Ilken and I were returning from a successful business development meeting with a major client. We had convinced him to let us handle a major chunk of his investment portfolio.

"I am contemplating investing some of this money in setting up Married Homes. I think they will do really well."

"Married Homes?" I admitted finally, after trying to tax the gray cells in vain. "I'm not sure I get what you mean, Boss."

"They shall be on the same lines as Old Age Homes . . . to which people can retire once they get married and live happily ever after." He rambled on in an unguarded and contemplative manner all through the drive back to the office.

Mr Mike M. Ilken was really quite upbeat about my perform-ance as a marketer that day. In fact, that was the evening when he walked into my office without warning and handed over a really neat Toshiba laptop computer. It was beautifully gift-wrapped and had a note clipped to the warranty card that said, "*From Tokyo with Love—Toshi San.*"

"This" he said, as I unwrapped it, "is the ultimate life companion. It fits snugly into your lap, exudes warmth when you switch it on, never gains weight, never has body odour or bad breath, never complains, argues or talks back, always helps you do your work and corrects your grammatical and spelling errors in a most inoffensive manner, is not susceptible to menopause or mid-life crises, can be easily and periodically upgraded, responds to touch, can be turned on or off with just one finger and, the best part is, if it starts to misbehave you can just reboot it."

Having handed over Toshi San to me with a flourish and bestowed on me a paternal smile as he saw my obvious pleasure, he turned to leave when his eye fell on the poster I had placed near my cabin door. The poster had an angel in white floating through the clouds and a caption below her that said,

If you can imagine it
You can achieve it.

With a hearty laugh he picked up a permanent marker from my table and below the caption added the words,

Only if you relentlessly work at it!
Perseverance pays!!

Tossing the marker back to me with yet another knowing, paternal smile he left my office.

Further recognition of Boss's pleasure came when he called me to his office the very next week and told me that he was planning to take the company national.

"I like the way you think, boy. You remind me of myself when I was young. Just remember that to succeed in life you have to be like Arjun.[1] Remain totally focused on the target at all times." He waved me to a seat. "Now, getting down to the business at hand, I want you to run point for me and help me put this company on the country's map."

"Thank you so much, Boss." I was quite thrilled with all this praise and deeply touched to be involved in such a prestigious project. "You can bank on me to do my very best and live up to your expectations. I shall never let you down, Boss."

There was a rather long pause before he replied. "Model, my son," he seemed rather pleased, yet at the same time, I noted a strange sadness shroud him, "I know you mean well and speak from your heart, but a voice within tells me that not far in the future you shall deny me thrice."

Me. Indignantly. "Boss! That voice within has got it all wrong. It must be confusing me for someone else. I shall *never* deny thee."

"That, my son, time alone will tell." He shakes his head, snaps out of the blue mood he has momentarily fallen into and returns to the moment. "Right. Now I want you to take a week and come up with a detailed battle plan."

"Okay, Boss. I'll get down to it right away."

"Good! And since you are going to be riding point for us, let me point you in the right direction."

---

[1] Despite the fact that a lot of feminists don't think much of him, Arjun was a very focused dude. For more about him, please read the *Mahabharat*.

"Sure, Boss." I promptly open my Day Timer and get ready with the trusty old pencil.

"Do you know what an army does and how it functions, Model?"

"Of course I do, Boss." I point my pencil in a militant manner. "They fight."

"That's right boy. But the Army does not just fight. They fight to win. And do you know how they do that? They keep the plan simple so that it is easy to implement. They keep everything absolutely focused on the aim that has to be achieved. THAT is how they win. Got it?"

"I got that, Boss," I reply, having dutifully noted it all down.

"Good! So you also make sure your plan is firmly and singularly focused on the aim. *Make sure that each and every resource is totally committed towards our aim.*"

"Yes, Boss! I remember what you told me—I am going to be like Arjun."

"Good boy!" He replied, much moved by my enthusiasm. "This is what I want you to do. First, lay down a simple system that will deliver a quality product to our customer. Second, create a system that monitors this system and catches problems as they arise, because every system is prone to failure and human error. Third, ensure you have a command and control element that performs a predictive function so that we can plan ahead, try to foresee problems and identify opportunities as early as possible. Got it?"

"I think so, Boss," I replied after I had jotted down all this.

"Way to go, kid!" Boss points a three-fingered pistol at me and bids me adieu. I close the Day Timer, straighten my tie and exit after saluting smartly.

I spend the whole of the next week burning kilolitres of midnight oil as I agonise over the problem of which cities to select, the layout of the offices, staffing pattern and a host of such issues.

Finally, after much deliberation, I put together my presentation and land up at the Boss's office on the designated morning.

"Come on in," Boss calls out when I knock. When I enter he is mulling over a map of the country mounted on the wall facing his chair. "Got the plans, Model?"

"Yes, Boss," I reply as I power up Toshi San, swivel her to ensure Boss has a clear view of the screen and then click on the first slide. "These are the cities I have selected, Boss."

Boss gives the list a cursory look. "I don't think you got the cities right, boy. Here . . . these are the cities we will begin with."

Swivelling his chair suddenly, faster than Dusty Fog, Boss unleashes six darts at the map of the country mounted on the far wall. The darts smoke across the room like greased lightening and thump into the map with decisive thwacks.

"*Mama mia*," I heard Boss whisper as he preened and blew imaginary smoke off his fingers, "They didn't call me the fastest dart in Dadri for nothing."

Me. Totally impressed with Boss's decisiveness and the flamboyant manner in which it was communicated; yet a trifle miffed that he was making me work on something that he had already made up his mind about.

"Yes, Boss. But don't you think that these two areas," I point at two of the still quivering darts, "are not as fertile as these two?" I point with the laser pointer towards two cities that had been on my list.

Boss gives a patient nod. "Son, you have yet to understand that there is no such thing as fertile or infertile. It is up to us to make the area fertile." Dramatic pause. "In any case, maybe next time the darts will seek out the cities you recommend." Another dramatic pause, as he blew some more imaginary smoke off his fingers. "My darts never strike the same place twice." Yet another dramatic pause.

"In any case when we are about to conquer the world does it matter which city we take first? Next slide."

Swallowing my chagrin I caress the touch pad on Toshi San. She responds immediately by displaying the next slide. Pointing to the slide I continue.

"Boss, these are the factors we should consider when we are designing the layout of an office in any city."

That's when I realise that Boss is not looking at the slide. He is watching me instead. There is a strange, tolerant smile on his face. I am about to speak when he pre-empts me.

"Tell me Model, how long have you been going to the same barber?"

"Barber? Eh?" I am totally flabbergasted. "What the hell does a barber have to do with all this? I give him a long look. It suddenly strikes me that he is dead serious. I do a little mental calculation and then reply tentatively, "About eleven years, Boss. Why?"

"In these eleven years how many times have you shifted house?"

Tedious though the whole exercise is becoming, I do a little more mental mathematics. "I think thrice, Boss. Why?"

"How far was the barber's shop from your first house and how far is it now?"

"It was a two-minute walk from my first house, Boss, and now it is about a thirty-minute drive. But why are you asking me all this?" All this mental mathematics is making my head hurt.

"When you moved house why didn't you change your barber? Why didn't you look for one closer by? Is this barber really that good? Is he really worth the long drive?" Pause. "Think, Model, think carefully before you answer."

I did. I thought over the whole thing in great detail before I answered. "Boss, it is because this guy's salon is so much like the one where I used to get my hair cut when I was a kid. It's just that . . ." I searched for the right words for a moment, "it is a very familiar and comforting atmosphere for me . . . I feel very comfortable and relaxed there . . . you get the point, don't you, Boss?"

"Model, my dear Model, of course I do. I know exactly what you mean." He waved magnanimously. "Very few people consciously realise that no man wishes to change his Bank, his Barber or his Brothel willingly. These are the three Big B's in a man's life and they have a very special significance."

He gave a brief pause, to allow me to ponder over the depth of this profound wisdom and then continued in a slow, earnest manner.

"You see, Model, to the lay person a company like ours is as good as a bank. This is where he comes to put his money, to make it work for him. He trusts us. Now, if you think carefully, you will realise that we all tend to relax and let our guard down when we are in a familiar environment. To put our clients' minds to rest, to make them relax and let their guard down, we have to create the same calm and familiar atmosphere at all our branches. The model we have used at the Head Office has proved to be highly successful. Thus every branch office will be an exact replica of the Head Office, though of course the size of the office and staff would be proportionate to the size of the city." He gave a dramatic pause. "Remember our aim, Model. Our aim is to make people feel relaxed and comfortable so that they hand over their money to us without any major selling effort on our part. So, *think global, but act focused.*"

Thus it came about that no matter which city you went to we were watching your back in pretty much the same manner. In fact, things reached such a state that several employees and clients even complained that their holidays had been ruined when they came across our branch office in some remote and exotic city.

"We were so struck by the similarity that we started feeling we had never even left our hometowns," they came carping.

To give him due credit, Mr Mike M. Ilken dismissed such stuff as asinine and baseless. He stuck to his SSDD[2] policy without batting an eyelid. And, to give credit where it is due, he was proved right, since every office reported that money was pouring in. The company coffers were filling up faster than our think tank could deploy the money.

It was when I was about to leave for the second round of expansion that Boss decided I needed a professional media person to help me build the company's brand and image. That's when he called me in to his office again. He was on the phone when I entered. He just gave me a brief look and muttered, "Please hold on for a moment," to whoever was at the other end. Then cupping the receiver he spoke to me. "Model, come in, come in, my man. Meet Mary." He gestured towards the couch at the other end of his office. "She is the VP who shall be handling all media-related matters. She is a very focused person and comes highly recommended. I want the two of you to spearhead the company's expansion drive. Now you guys get to know each other while I finish this call." Then he went back to talking on the phone.

I barely heard all this because my mind had ceased to function the minute I turned and saw Mary. "*Mother of God!*" I felt the thought race through my head. *She is so beautiful . . . so immaculate . . . .*

There was something about Mary. Don't ask me what, how or why. I have no clue. I just know that the minute I set eyes on her

[2] The "SSDD" here stands for "Same Style Duplicate Design" and must not be confused with the hick/crappy (Same Shit Different Day) version of the acronym.

I knew she was *the* one I had been waiting for all my life. I think (in fact I am quite sure) the feeling was mutual for she was also looking at me with unblinking eyes and bated breath.

As luck would have it, I could be reasonably sure that (keeping in view WATCH YOUR BACK's singles-only policy) she was legally single, if not fully unattached. Thus I was spared the aggravation of watching my back against jealous husbands. All this passed through my mind at the speed of thought, as our gazes locked together like Luke Skywalker's light sabre. Luckily Boss was too preoccupied with his phone call to notice anything. He just glanced up briefly to say, "Right then, I will leave you two to get on with it," and as we were leaving he waved us off with a gay, "Don't do anything I wouldn't."

The very second we were out of his office I turned to her and asked, "What's your status? Are you single?" I just had to be sure, you see.

"I am single and I'm a virgin," Mary murmured to me with a shy smile in her eyes. "I think I have been waiting for you all my life." Her smile deepened as I heaved a sigh of relief and pleasure.

Till date I am pretty sure that neither Mary nor I have any clue as to how the rest of the day went by or what we talked about. I do know that (as per Boss's orders) we got on with it pretty quick. The chemistry was so strong that biology could hardly be far behind. That evening as we made wild, passionate love at my place we were pretty sure that we were doing things Boss wasn't.

The next few weeks passed in a blur. It was all sex and the city. A lot of the former and quite a bit of the latter. I remember the sex clearly but am not too sure of the city. I do know that it was only when we were about to open the fourth or fifth branch office that trouble first reared its ugly head between Mary and me.

"You are not your usual bright and chirpy self," I said to her as we were walking in for the press conference that followed the inauguration ceremony. "You seem distraught and de-focused."

She just shrugged and mumbled something under her breath.

As soon as the press conference was over I hustled her to the newly finished conference hall.

"What is the problem, Mary?" I asked. "Please talk to me."

However, no matter how hard I tried to get to the bottom of things she just wouldn't open up and talk. In fact, that whole day and the rest of the night I was unable to get to the bottom of anything. Mary had gone to ground like a good infantry soldier under fire.

The very next day we both moved to the next city that had been fortunate enough to have Boss's dart land on it. With the inauguration of the city office only about a week away, there was a load of workmen giving finishing touches to a load of things. The humming of saws, the grating of cutting machines, the teeth-shattering whine of polishing machines and the constant hammering of carpenters percolated through the atmosphere.

As was by now the norm, Mary and I ended up in the office of the City Manager. I immediately noticed that the city map mounted on hardboard was missing.

"Where is the city map that is supposed to be on the wall?" I asked the city manager. "You don't want to miss the opportunity to display your leadership skills and decisiveness while briefing the sales team every morning? Do you now?"

"Oops!" The city manager ran to have the omission rectified.

A couple of hours of feedback, review of the situation and brainstorming the problems that existed saw us get the project on track.

The city bumpkins left us head-office types alone as they went off to complete the pending jobs. Mary and I finally got to put our feet up and let our hair down with a cup of coffee and a burger.

"So, how is the burger?"

"Well, I'm not exactly loving it, but I am so hungry that it will do," Mary replied picking at the burger absently.

"Quite." Pause. Not very happy as I took another bite out of my Happy Meal. "So? Are you going to tell me what is bugging you?"

Mary. Very softly and hesitantly. "I think I'm pregnant."

There was a moment of stunned silence before my "YIPPEEE" scorched through the yet-to-be inaugurated city office, bringing pause even to the relentless carpenter hammering away somewhere. Mary, jerking forward with a start and making shushing gestures, "Hush! Don't shout like that, people will wonder what's up."

"I don't care. I'm so happy." I am stiff armed to a stop as I rush forward to hug her.

"What are you doing for God's sake? Anyone can walk in any time."

"I just don't care, Mary. I am so happy," I reply ecstatically.

"Happy! What the hell are you happy about? I'm pregnant! Boss will start having kittens if I start having babies? Do you realise what this will do to my goals and ambitions?"

"To hell with the boss and to goals and ambitions, Mary," I wave vehemently. "They are only as important as we want them to be. Success is what we perceive it to be. Work, promotion and monetary success are not the be-all and end-all of life. Let us get married, Mary."

"Married?" She looks at me incredulously. "Are you nuts? Boss will throw us out before you can say 'I do.' Everything that I have worked for will go down the drain."

She paused as though searching for the right words.

"I agree Model, that success is what we perceive it to be, but you must understand that the goals we set for ourselves are landmarks to let us know we are still on the path that we have chosen. No matter how small or insignificant they may seem to others, but every time we attain a goal that we have set for ourselves it does give us happiness and a sense of achievement. Please understand, Model . . . attaining these goals is important for me and I can only do that if I stay on the path and refuse to get diverted. The minute I lose focus I will lose sight of my goals, Model."

There was a catch in her voice and I could see that she was trying very hard not to cry.

"They may be illusions, but they are the illusions we live for. If we let our illusions die, we also cease to exist. Model, please . . . *please* try to understand."

I was totally torn up inside. I couldn't believe it was my Mary saying all this to me.

"Mary, *Mary*, *please* listen to me. Success and happiness are not co-dependent. We can be miserable even when we are successful. Conversely, we can be happy without being what we deem as successful. Please do not walk away from a chance to be happy . . . that would be the original sin . . . you know we go so well together."

Mary shook her head gently, but firmly as she replied. "I do not know what sin it will be Model, but I *do* know that I will be miserable if I do not attain my aims. I must achieve what I have strived so hard for . . . please try to understand, Model. Even if

I am unable to, I shall at least have the comfort of knowing that I gave it my best shot. But if I walk away from my goals now, I will always carry the regret for the rest of my life."

She tugged at my arm.

"I do want to be with you, but I know that I will end up blaming you for taking me away from my dreams. Especially now when they are just within touching reach."

I was so agitated that it took all my self-control to stop myself from reaching out and shaking her. "Listen, I understand what you are saying . . . I respect your need to achieve, but we need to adapt to what life throws at us. At times we need to change track. We can still come back to our chosen paths later. We are going to have a baby and I think we owe it to the kid to get married. Boss can take a dive for all I care."

Mary's tone was firm. "No Model. We cannot keep changing tracks all the time. This much I have learnt . . . *in life, diversions, irritants and opportunities never end.* They will keep emerging and beckoning to us. Every so often another little path will emerge. There will always be compelling reasons for me to take yet another small diversion. I do not know which path is right or wrong, but I do know that once we lose sight of the goal it is hard, if not impossible, to return to the path that leads us to it. If I have a baby at this point of time, my career will be shot to hell . . . not to mention what Boss is going to say about it."

"Boss! Boss!! Boss!!!" I was fuming with rage by now. "Who cares? We can always move to a faraway land, get other jobs and live happily ever after."

The rest of the day passed by as we argued back and forth, but nothing decisive emerged. Nothing either one of us said seemed to have any impact on the other. That evening, for the first time since we had met, we slept in our own hotel rooms.

When there was a sharp knock on the door the next morning I assumed it was Mary. I rushed to the door to find one of the hotel guys there with a message slip.

I would like to meet Mary and you at the City Office at 10:00 hours. Sharp. Mike. M. Ilken.

That's what the note said. I was a bit surprised by Boss's sudden appearance on the scene but not perturbed, since Boss was known to land up unannounced. I passed on the message to Mary while we were mournfully going through the eggs, bacon and juice. She gave a guilty start and then lapsed into a sullen silence. I attributed the whole thing to hormonal changes taking place inside her and was sure that she would come around with time and all would be well in the end.

When we walked into the city office, the workmen were still going at it hammer and tongs. I could hear the relentless carpenter hammering away without pause. Boss did not say a word to us when he walked in a moment later. He headed straight to the conference room. When we followed him in, he just acknowledged our "good mornings" with a faint nod of his head and then motioned for us to sit down. Then he pulled out his pipe, filled it, tamped it and lit it. That apparently was a covert signal for someone unseen who was watching us, for suddenly voices began to fill the room.

A look of sheer horror swamped our faces as Mary and I heard a recording of our conversation the previous evening fill the room. Mary and I sat through the whole thing in total silence with our heads bowed. The silence continued long after the recording had run out.

Finally, Boss looked up. His eyes were like bullets as they gored into me. The unflinching stare seemed to last an eternity. When he finally spoke there was huge sorrow in his voice.

"Did I not tell thee Model that thrice you shall deny me? The voice within was right. It has never misled me and never shall."

I had barely started to mumble my humble apologies when the Boss's upraised hand stopped me.

"Model! Don't say anything. I forgive you your trespasses, but I will not allow you to stay on. It would set an unacceptable precedence if I allowed such gross indiscipline to go unpunished." I think there was a faint hint of tears in his eyes, but they did not shake his determination. "I hereby banish you from WATCH YOUR BACK for ever more. Do not come to the office again. We shall have your belongings and dues sent to you."

Having said this he strode out.

After a moment's pause, so did Mary. She left without a word to me. By the time I reached the hotel she had checked out and left for the airport. I raced after her, but despite my most valiant efforts I was unable to catch the flight she was on.

By the time I took the next flight home, Mary had gone underground. All calls to her home and her mobile phone went unanswered. A lock on her apartment door greeted me every time I went there. The seventh time when I went to Mary's house her roommate reluctantly called me in.

"Mary has asked me to let you know that she is not going to meet you or take any calls from you."

"Why?" I was shocked. "Why can't she at least let me speak to her?"

The roommate shook her head gravely. "She has decided to retain her single status so that she does not get diverted from the aim she has selected for herself." She hesitated for a moment, then plunged ahead. Her voice speeded up as she spoke, as though she just wanted to say it and get it over with. "Last week Mary aborted the foetus and retained her job at WATCH YOUR BACK. In fact, she has been promoted and is now looking after your portfolio also."

Her words struck home like hammer blows, leaving me devastated and empty inside. A sharp painful despair flooded through me filling up the hollowness.

As I was returning weak and desolate from her house, the Third Commandment struck home like a thunderbolt—

Thou Shalt Remain Firmly Focused on the Selected Aim

I knew that this had to be the Lord's way of telling me that one could only succeed if one remained firmly focused on it.

Much as the whole thing hurt me, somewhere deep inside I think I understood Mary's decision to remain focused on something she wanted to achieve. We all have the right to decide what we want from our lives and then work with single-minded focus to achieve it. No matter where the chosen path eventually leads, at least we will have the satisfaction of knowing that we gave our best shot to what we really wanted to do.

Isn't that what Life is all about?

At the time of taking it, no one can know if a decision is right or wrong. That time alone will tell. But I do know that once we have selected an aim for ourselves, we can achieve it *only* if we stick to the path that leads to it, without flinching.

Deeply wounded but much wiser, I decided to continue my solitary trek on the Lord's learning curve.

- *Brilliance, education and hard work; everything may fail, but perseverance always pays.*

- *Always have a clear aim in life and select interim goals that lead to this aim.*

- *Every time you achieve an interim goal you shall enjoy the happiness of knowing you have succeeded and are still on the path to your selected aim.*

- *Life will keep presenting you with distractions, attractions, irritants and opportunities that beckon and tempt you to stray from the path that leads to the selected goal or divert resources that you need to achieve the selected aim.*

- *Stay focused—it helps you to succeed.*

Thus spake Model . . .

M.O.D.E.L.'s *Fourth Commandment*

Month Eleven and Day Eleven P.D.A.

Thus spake Model . . .

I felt no anguish at my departure from WATCH YOUR BACK, since I had always known that it was merely a matter of time before the Lord delivered the wisdom of the Third Commandment unto me and I would have to move on to fresher pastures.

However Mary's departure from my life left a terrible void within me. I felt as though all happiness had been sucked out of me. Intense pain became a part of my existence. For many moons I mooned and mused over what might have been had she said yes and become a part of my life. Till this day I remember the pain and often wish the Lord had chosen a less painful way to deliver His priceless wisdom to me.

Maybe the Lord also appreciated my anguish for He granted me a short sabbatical to drink myself silly; to blank out the confused medley of emotions that thronged through my mind; the agony (of losing Mary) and the ecstasy (of having discovered the wisdom of yet another commandment).

Five full working days went by before the lady from the Lord's consulting firm called me. I noticed that this time she did not ask me why I had left WATCH YOU BACK. I guess the Lord was gently guiding her. Or maybe, she had received a call from WATCH YOUR BACK and was steering clear of such a delicate matter.

"If you are looking for another opening we have a wonderful slot at the BPO named ENOCH. I took the liberty of discussing your profile with them and they are quite keen on meeting with you . . . tomorrow . . . if that is fine with you."

"It is fine with me," I replied with all the enthusiasm I could muster. Thereupon she gave me the contact details and the address. I dutifully jotted them down.

"Did you get all that?" She asked, a lot more gently than was her wont. I guess she must have felt the pain in my voice, much as I tried to maintain a stiff upper lip and mask it. When I murmured an affirmative she uttered a gentle "Good!" and hung up.

What on earth will I do at a BPO? I wondered. *I know absolutely nothing about them, except that they process stuff at the back.*

Not that I was overly worried, since I knew that I would get the job because that was the will of the Lord. Sure enough I did. Barely had the ink dried on the appointment letter, I was carting in my cardboard carton and settling down in the cabin allotted to me.

It was at ENOCH that I met Cain. He was the guy I was going to replace in that company.

I had barely settled in my new cabin when I heard a loud assertive knock on the door. Before I could respond the door flew ajar and in strode this massive, burly guy with a huge and highly infectious smile plastered all over his face.

"HI!" said he, striding up to me with his hand extended. "Welcome to ENOCH, Brother Model. I'm Cain." The handshake was as firm and reassuring as the smile. "I am the one who is going to hand over charge of my duties to you. 'Tis my humble lot to make you familiar with the ways of ENOCH."

Frankly, I was quite overawed by the sheer size and aura of his presence and was trying hard to recover my mental footing.

Nevertheless I did manage to make the right motions and mumble the required pleasantries.

Now this Cain, who was to be the Lord's instrument at this fourth halt on the divine learning curve, was (and remains to this day) a bright, colourful and hail-fellow-well-met kind of guy, always full of jokes and a smile for everyone. Our paths crossed for but thirty days in which Cain handed over charge to me while he completed his notice period with ENOCH.

These thirty days were momentous to say the least and were to have an extraordinary effect on my life. In retrospect this also turned out to be one of the most pleasurable of all the labours that the Lord assigned to me.

With basic courtesies behind us, Cain decided that the best way to move forward and hand over his charge to me was for him to take me around ENOCH and let me meet the inhabitants. We had barely left the cabin and were heading for the cafeteria when a harried looking young man hurried up to us and accosted Cain.

"Sir, a huge problem has come up," he blurted out a trifle breathlessly, "one of the customer service supervisors just got into an altercation with a client. She is very miffed and raising Cain . . . I beg your pardon sir . . . she is yelling her head off and threatening all kinds of things . . . I tell you sir, we have such idiots in Customer Relations . . . they are always creating silly hassles for us . . . ."

Cain had been hearing him out with a gentle smile thus far. He now reached out and placed a soothing hand on his shoulder.

"Calm down brother . . . take a deep breath, count to ten . . . collect yourself and breathe deeply."

He then led him back into the cabin and offered him a chair.

"Now listen . . . these things are bound to happen. We are dealing with human beings and they are prone to cut loose from time to time. That is why we have managers. To step in and take charge when things go awry. *It is human to err, my boy. It is managerial to resolve."*

The young manager was quite agitated and about to butt in, but Cain held up a polite yet firm hand.

"Listen to me, young Lancelot. Listen and learn or sorry will be your lot. This is what I want you to do. Go down and meet the lady who is upset, make her sit in the conference room, get her some water and tea and allow her to vent her rage. Hear her out fully and when she is done apologise to her. Assure her that we have nothing except her best interests at heart and we shall take requisite action against the concerned individual. After you have done that call the customer relations' supervisor to your cabin and have a word with him. Make it clear to him that he must not be overly emotional whilst on the job and be more guarded in his speech. There are many ways to communicate one's displeasure without being abusive. He has to learn to be polite and yet firm. Have you got that?"

"Yes, sir, I have," young Lancelot answered with some traces of agitation still evident in his tone, "but what if she doesn't calm down or listen to me. . . ."

"Boy! Just do what I tell you to do. She will calm down and she will listen. An upset customer is always full of sound and fury and it all signifies nothing if you allow it to be dissipated. Remember that they also don't need this aggro and are equally eager to have the whole issue resolved ASAP. Boy, life is so full of hassles . . . who needs more. However, if she doesn't listen give me a call. Okay? I will come down and take care of it."

With that Cain sent him off, making soothing noises as Lancelot went. When the door had closed shut behind him, he turned to me.

"Lancelot is a good lad, but a bit too easily flustered. Time and exposure will temper the steel in him."

I murmured something non-committal and then asked, "Don't you think you should have gone down and handled her yourself rather than expose her to a nervous young manager. With your experience, are you not better poised to handle the matter? He may well agitate her even more and then you will be left with a bigger mess to clean up."

"No, no brother Model. If I did that wee Lancelot will never learn to stand on his own feet and work independently. I know for a fact that he is far more capable than he thinks he is. We must give him the opportunity to grow to his potential. Most of us are so fond of rushing in, taking charge and leading the way that we do not allow people working under us to flourish and attain their true potential. It is far more important for ENOCH, Lancelot and me to have him gain knowledge and experience than for me to handle the problem, since it is certain that I cannot be present at every place where there is a problem. No? Even if he leaves me with a bigger mess . . . what the hell . . . that's what they pay me for, right?"

Having said that he kind of mentally brushed his hands and then looked at me, "Should we resume our journey, my friend?" and led the way to the cafeteria.

I followed him, rather sheepishly I might add.

ENOCH was a veritable beehive of activity. Due to the nature of the work, which I was still to try and understand fully, the average age of people thronging its corridors was rather on the younger side. Consequently extreme enthusiasm and electric energy seemed to stalk unchecked.

Every once in a while some young bundle of nervous energy would accost Cain and unload some problem or other on him.

Once in a while Cain would even walk up to some people he saw in distress and query them gently about what ailed them.

I watched in awe and silence as Cain heard them out and then calmed them down. Invariably they would leave much relieved and full of resolve to solve whatever it is that had been vexing them. We were scouting the second floor when young Lancelot caught up with us again.

"Sir . . . Cain . . ." his features were awash with a satisfied smile as he fell upon us like a flash flood. "I got the whole darned mess resolved. I had that lady eating out of my hand by the time I was done with her. As for that customer relations guy . . . you can bet that he will relate better with customers henceforth. I gave him a piece of my mind and he left my cabin quite contrite and over-flowing with remorse."

I am quite sure that Lancelot would have waxed eloquent for quite a while had Cain not interjected gently.

"Good show! I am proud of you lad. Never for a moment did I doubt that you would not succeed."

Lancelot beamed like a halogen lamp at Halloween.

"Gee! Really, Boss?"

Cain patted him paternally on the back. "Of course, dear boy. You have so much potential. That is why we bank on you so heavily."

For one fleeting moment I had a feeling that Cain was overdoing it, but then I realised that Lancelot was plagued by no such misgivings. He literally bloomed with the praise and there was a noticeable swagger in his walk as he strode away.

If I thought this show had been put on to impress me, that illusion was rapidly dispelled in the days that followed. In fact the very next day when we were again doing our rounds of ENOCH, as we were passing by the Control Room, the young lady on duty there saw us and rushed out.

"Sir . . . sir . . ." she called out to Cain, and when he turned, "I have finished the work you had wanted me to do. Would you please have a look at it?"

Cain gave her an approving nod, "Of course I will have a look at it! Lead the way, kindly light."

Cain walked into the Control Room with me in tow and spent a few long minutes going over the documents she had produced for him. Every once in a while he would give a nod and once in a while a solemn "hmm" exited from his lips.

Finally he turned to her, "Let me tell you, dear lady, you are doing a good job here. The pride you take in your work is evident. But don't you realise that *the difference in effort required in doing something, doing it well and doing it excellently is so marginal* that I am surprised you should settle for just good work. You have the potential to do much better."

She beamed. He gave her a final approving nod and headed for the door. As we were about to exit he paused and turned to the lady again.

"Let me tell you three things that will hold you in good stead no matter where you go or what you do. Every morning when you start for work, just stop for a moment and ask yourself, *'What is the one thing that I'm going to do better today than I did yesterday.'* And then, in the evening when you lie down and muse over the day gone by, just ask yourself two questions, *'What new thing did I learn today?'* and *'Which person did I teach something to today?'* "

Cain gave a pause while he waited for her to absorb this.

"Rest assured that this little introspection would transform the quality of your life and of those around you."

With that Cain moved on. Soon the hustle and bustle of ENOCH surrounded us again. I followed in mute silence, letting his words sink in.

And so the saga continued. Every day I saw Cain walk into a mess of problems where maniacal managers, screaming supervisors, woebegone workers and clamouring customers rend at each other. Invariably, he would walk away leaving behind calmer people resolving problems in a saner manner.

Cain never seemed to loose his cool. No matter how grossly the other person had erred or messed up, Cain would invariably find something to praise her or him about. In fact Cain would make it a point to find something that the person was good at or had done well and then use that to spur her/him on in the right direction.

Each such episode left me filled with greater doubts about my capability to stand in Cain's shoes and fill the gap his departure would leave behind. In fact, such was the power of his persona that it started giving me shivers just to think how I would manage; especially since people, being what they are, always tend to remember only the good things from the past and would always hold me up in comparison.

I was planning to speak to him and seek his guidance, but somehow we never seemed to get any time alone. Something or other kept coming up to prevent me from having a tête-à-tête with him. That is why I was pretty surprised when by sheer coincidence I ran into Cain at Noah's Ark that very evening.

Noah's Ark was the name of the bar, located just a stone's throw from ENOCH, where all the Marketing types would hang around. It was a quaint bar with a truly escapist attitude. It was made of gopher wood and was about three hundred cubits long, fifty cubits wide and thirty cubits high. It had this one really HUGE window and a door set to the side thereof. In many ways it was like the quarterdeck of one of the ancient wooden boats that we see in old movies on Romans and Trojans (the horse guys, not the condom chaps) and stuff.

The best thing about the Ark was that it always seemed to have a place for everyone. Nobody ever got bounced out of the Ark. They had this "*if the Good Lord has sent you to the Ark, the Good Lord shall provide (space) for you here*" attitude. It was perpetually crowded since it always had the "Happy Hours" sign hanging outside and was quite easy on the pocket.

The Ark was totally unlike Heaven, the really swish and modernist place right next door. The prices in Heaven were enough to submerge us poor folks. The loud techno music there left one hearing-challenged in a very short while. Most Marketing and Customer Relations types hated that place. We couldn't hear ourselves think there, let alone talk. That was what turned most of us off. I mean can you imagine a Marketing or Customer Relations bloke who doesn't want to hear the sound of his/her own voice. Heaven was where all these cyber nerds hung out. They are so used to not talking in any case.

Our bar was also totally unlike the dimly lit and tomb-like place called Judas on the other side. It had this really horrendous facade and no music at all. So, we were in the middle—Heaven, the techno place was on the right and Judas, the other tomblike place, was on the left.

Judas was known as the lawyers' haunt. They were about the only ones who frequented the place. Lawyers and the really dumb 'touristy' types who didn't know any better. Though I always wanted to check it out—just to get an idea of what it is that passes for social conversation amongst lawyers. I mean do they talk about *torts, locus standi, ipso facto* and passing motions and decrees and stuff? But curious as I was I could never rake up the nerve to go there. Lawyers petrify me. Anyway, let me not wander off the story.

That evening, I was safely ensconced in the Ark, squished in between this couple, a male and a female, who seemed about to couple. But their antics bothered me not, since such things flourished freely in the Ark and we had all been trained to mind our own business.

So, there I was, lost happily in my thoughts as I sat communing with Brother Bacchus when all of a sudden someone gave me a real hard thump on my back.

"Hey! Well met by the moonlight Proud Model. Good to see you here! How goest thou brother?"

I turned to set my eyes on Cain and a welcome sight it was, for in truth, scintillating though Brother Bacchus' company is, it does tend to get boring after some time. Also, like I had mentioned earlier, Cain was looming large in my mind these days and happy was I to meet him again, especially in such an informal setting.

"Cain! My dear chap! What a pleasant surprise. You come most carefully upon your hour. Come, come, pull a log and sit thee down."

(We all called those wooden bar stools that liberally littered the Ark as "logs".)

Thereafter followed some really enthralling and entertaining conversation, for Cain was a downright jovial chap and so full of life. Then, once the initial exuberance had abated a mite, Cain gave me a long look and asked, "Why art thou stressed out? And why is thy countenance fallen? Why be there dark circles under thine eyes?"

"In sooth I know not why I am so wearied. It's just the pressures of work, I guess. You know how it is in the first few weeks. There are so many new things and so much to catch up on."

"Is that all, my dear friend," Cain asked me gently, yet in a most penetrating manner. "If it is so, then all I can say is don't let the pressure get to you. *Take things one at a time and pace them out so that you can do each of them in a manner befitting your style and standards.* That will take the pressure off you and also give you the satisfaction of being able to do things excellently."

"I know what you mean Cain, but it is not that . . . I would be more than happy to just do things well . . . ."

"But, why . . ." Cain interjected gently, "why should you accept anything but the excellent. You of all people should set the highest standard; especially for yourself so that the others around you follow your example. I'm sure an experienced hand such as you is aware that leading by example is the best, if not the only, way to lead. No?"

"I know that Cain," I replied, not able to hold myself back any more, "but I am rather worried about my ability to hold the fort in the manner that you have been doing at ENOCH all this while. I am afraid that I will always be compared to you and found wanting."

"Compared to me! And found wanting!" Cain gave me an amazed look. He seemed genuinely surprised. "And here I was looking up to you, wondering what you think of me." He gave a short laugh. "Isn't it strange that we are able to see the strengths and potential of others so easily and yet not realise our own."

"I'm not kidding, Cain."

"No, Model, neither am I. What is so special about me that you need to worry about having to live up to?"

"Can you not see Cain, how easily and effectively you are able to motivate people around you and get them to perform to the very best of their ability?"

"Oh that!" Cain laughed, not offensively I might add. He seemed genuinely pleased. "That's nothing. I just focus on harnessing their strengths and trying to help them overcome their weaknesses. That's all."

"*That's all*! Good Lord, Cain, don't you realise that this is the very key that we all seek. All of us go through life trying to get those around us, especially those working for us, to perform to the best of their ability. And let me tell you, not many of us succeed.

We are so busy trying to score brownie points and so easily threatened by the success of others that we seldom try to bring out the best in them. On the contrary, we even derive sadistic pleasure in the failures of others and in running them down."

"But getting the best out of people is so easy Model. All we have to do is to remember that most people never realise their true potential. The few who do, never get the opportunity to live up to it. Most of us live through life having to work under managers who always focus on our shortcomings and seldom utilise our strengths. When I realised this I swore to myself that I would always seek out the best in people. That's all that I do now. *I believe that given the opportunity people will rise and outperform their own expectations if we can make them believe in themselves and keep on training them.*"

"But Cain, if we only focus on their strengths and do not correct them and help them to overcome their weaknesses, don't we do them a disservice? Are we not preventing them from improving?"

"I agree with you, brother Model. I don't ignore their weaknesses, but I prefer to approach them from a positive direction. I like to help them overcome their weaknesses by making them believe that they can, rather than forcing or criticising them to improve. We have to train them by allowing them to experience and support them with the learning of our own experiences."

Cain paused and gave me a long look. He hesitated for a moment before he spoke.

"Just look at you, Model . . . you are so smartly dressed, so well organised and so focused on what you want to do . . . I have envied you from the very minute I set eyes on you."

"Me?" I was genuinely surprised. "What is so special about me? I am not able to motivate my team the way you do. You give them so much freedom and space to work in and so much support when they go wrong."

"But Model, what else can I do? You see, my success and my performance are directly proportional to how well they perform. Since I cannot be everywhere myself I have to make sure that they are well trained, upbeat and trying to do better than they have been doing so far. I just help them to succeed, by being there for them to fall back on. Isn't that what managers are supposed to do?" Cain replied. And I could see that there was nothing but honest curiosity flowing through him as he looked at me quizzically.

"That is so true, Cain," I replied after pondering about it for a while. "You are so right . . . all of us are so scared of doing badly and so unwilling and untrusting of others' abilities that we just butt in and take charge at the first sign of trouble. *We never allow them to grow, to experience, and to learn.*"

There was a long silence as we pondered over all that had been said.

"You are right, Cain. *To succeed we have to ensure that those around us live up to their potential and succeed first.*"

We paused as the waitress came to our table. We both watched her rather closely, especially when she bent over to thump down two more beers in front of us, because her low-cut dress attracted male eyes the way a long-haired dog attracts fleas. She thumped down the mugs so hard that some of the beer spilled out onto the table. Despite this there was no change in the surly expression on her face. On the contrary, she had that I-dare-you-to-say-something expression all over her face. We were both watching her walk away when Cain spoke.

"Did you see that?"

I nodded vigorously. "Of course I did!" I said enthusiastically. "I couldn't help but do so, Cain. Her dress was cut rather low."

"No, no, I didn't mean that," Cain admonished gently, giving me a please-grow-up look. "Did you note how she thumped the beers down? That is one lady who is just going through the motions. She takes no pride or pleasure in her work."

"Maybe she doesn't enjoy being a waitress," I told him. "I know Confucius wanted all of us to choose a job we love so that we will never have to work even for a day, but I'm rather confused here, Cain, because more often than not things don't pan out the way we want them to and we often end up doing things just because we have no other options."

"I agree with you, Model, that things seldom go as planned, but the fact is that no matter what we choose to believe, none of us are ever without options. Yes, quite a few of us never find the courage to exercise those options.

"That's not very fair, Model. Most of us just struggle to complete our duties and discharge our obligations. We seldom have the time or energy to do what we really want to do.

"But of course, Model, I totally agree with you. But that does not alter the fact that we either need to find work that we like doing or become good at what we do whether we enjoy it or not. Take that lady here. . . ."

He pointed to the waitress who was busy thumping down more beers before the unsuspecting masses. "The efficiency quotient demonstrated by her is rather poor and its negative impact is enhanced by the fact that she thinks work is just another four-letter word. Consequently, she will never rise above being a surly waitress.

If she were to just smile a bit and show a little finesse in the way she serves people she would not only increase the size of the tip, she would be a happier human being and may soon end up as the bar supervisor or something."

"Oh . . . I see what you mean," I murmured sheepishly as I tore my eyes away from her and returned to gaze at Cain, rather impressed with the depth of his perception.

I do not know if it was the uplifting atmosphere of Noah's Ark or the fortifying beers in our hands, but Cain and I spent some very enriching hours engrossed in a most illuminating conversation that fateful eve. Consequently, after a very long time, there was a very noticeable joyous spring in my step when the Ark finally downed shutters for the night and we went our separate ways, homeward bound.

The spring in my step and confidence in my soul was even more evident the next morning when I clocked in at the office duly rested and recuperated. The power of positive thinking was pulsing through me. I knew there would be no problem in my being able to replace Cain at ENOCH; and maybe, God willing, I'd even do a better job. Very shortly the others around me knew it too.

That day not a soul left my presence without feeling a positive impact and no matter where I went I spread calm and contentment. In fact by mid-afternoon I suddenly realised that there was much less stress and anxiety all around and within me, even though problems persisted unabated.

By early evening I realised that my purpose here at ENOCH had been fulfilled. For the glory of the Lord's wisdom lay before me. I know the Fourth Commandment just had to be—

Thou Shalt always Seek Out the Best in People and Help Them Live Up to Their Potential

That very evening, just after Cain's farewell party, I walked across to the Managing Director and handed over my resignation.

"Why Model . . . . This is most surprising . . . what compelled thee to act so curiously?" he could not help blurting out.

I knew I could not reveal the truth to him. "I am very happy here at ENOCH but something personal has come up suddenly," I replied, simply. "It will not be possible for me continue, much as I would like to."

He looked so confused and troubled that my heart bled for him.

"I assure you that my services will be available to ENOCH till such time as you find a suitable replacement," I assured him.

"Oh . . . okay." Slightly mollified he went back to his musings.

I returned to the ruins of the party where a few people still hung around, picking at the cake and coffee in a half-hearted manner as they mused about life after Cain. I knew I had to cheer them up, so I called them around and spoke to them. "Remember, dear friends, Cain is moving on to better and brighter things. In any case, change is an inevitable part of life . . . it is essential for the show to go on."

By the time the second cup of coffee had been downed things were better and brighter. I left for home that evening with a light heart and a sense of fulfilment. And that is pretty much how I was feeling when I left the safe environs of ENOCH a few weeks later after passing on Cain's legacy to the bright-eyed youngster who replaced me. I was sorry to put ENOCH behind me, but I knew that duty called and my divine quest had to go on.

- *A chain is only as strong as the weakest link in it.*

- *Success is a team effort. We cannot succeed if we do not help others around us to succeed.*

- *People only live up to their potential if you make them believe in themselves, guide them with your experience and allow them to learn by experiencing.*

- *Given the opportunity people will always rise above and outperform their own expectations.*

- *Successful people help others to realise and live up to their true potential by helping them overcome their weaknesses*

- *Learning is a continuous and lifelong process.*

- *The difference in effort required to do something, to do it well, and to do it excellently is very marginal.*

- *Demonstrating efficiency is as important as actual efficiency.*

Thus spake Model . . .

M.O.D.E.L.'s *Fifth Commandment*

Month Fifteen and Day Nineteen P.D.A.

I think I must have been on the IT[1] and ITES[2] part of the divine learning curve at this time—since from ENOCH, a BPO, I moved to BABYLON, a dotcom. That is where the lady from the Lord's consulting firm told me my new assignment was, just a few hours after I exited ENOCH.

"Do you know what all I had to hear because you resigned in such a manner?" She seemed mighty miffed when she called. Methinks she had gotten an earful from the people at ENOCH. "Who the heck resigns at the farewell party of the person they have been hired to replace . . . it's . . . it's simply ridiculous."

"Look I understand." I took her angst in my stride. "But I had compelling personal reasons that did not allow me to continue there."

"What?" She asked, quite belligerently.

"I'm sorry, but I cannot discuss them with you. They're personal." I replied firmly. "They are between me and my God," I added, bringing her as close to the truth as I could.

She threw a *"Yeah right"* at me as she signed off.

---

[1] Information Technology.
[2] Information Technology Enabled Services.

Anyway, since I was now nearing the halfway mark of the ten labours the Lord had assigned me, I reported for duty to BABYLON with a keen sense of anticipation and eagerness—after the motions of an interview and the hiring documentation were over.

Situated on the banks of the now dry river that had once flowed through the city, BABYLON was this new dotcom venture being funded by a group of angel investors out of Zion. (Though why they call them "Angel Investors" is a bit beyond me since I always found these guys lurking around in the shadows and demanding their pound of flesh, which they politely referred to as Return on Investment. If you ask me the whole thing was rather sinister.)

You must remember that this was the day and age of the dotcom boom. They were blooming all over the place. Everyone was in a tearing hurry to jump on to the bandwagon and strike it rich. Multi-million dollar deals were signed on used tissue papers and restaurant napkins. Mergers and acquisitions were flooding the front pages of all the trade papers almost daily.

The atmosphere in this sector was electric beyond imagination. There was coffee, cigarettes and an aura of highly-strung nerves all over the place. Screaming matches broke out for the most trivial things.

"Why are you using my phone?"

"Well, you were chewing my pencil yesterday."

"That's because I caught you red-handed caressing my mouse."

"And it's okay for you to ogle at my screensaver?"

No reason was small enough not to fight about.

The BP of business plan was more sacrosanct than the BP of blood pressure, even though the latter was higher.

"It is all about footfalls, eyeballs and content." The Venture Capitalist *guru*s would tell everyone. All and sundry bowed before and paid homage at the altar of that elusive Goddess called Revenue Model. Stock Options were the Holy Offertory.

Everyone worried about everything. People who apparently should have had nothing to worry about found things to worry about. Even office boys, mail runners and the housekeeping staff worried about whether the company had enough C+++ trained personnel.

"Don't you think," they would go around telling each other, "we should now look to hire people who know more Java than they consume?"

Courier delivery boys worried about and discussed EPS[3] and NAV[4] with the security guards while they waited for the elevator to arrive. The frequency of bowel movements matched those of the Dow Jones. The intensity and frenzy of sexual encounters kept pace with the Sensex. To sum it up, everyone was tense and nervous all the time and everything was password protected, including entry to the restrooms.

Within a few days of checking in I realised that of all the people here it was the guys who looked after the facility who really took the brunt of it all. They were the ones who were always on call and whose productivity and efficiency was always under test and review.

At BABYLON, the Director Facilities was a guy called Abel. His cabin was just down the corridor from mine. Right outside the door to his office was this huge poster of some people cleaning up the office that said,

Wars are fought once in a rare while,
But administration goes on forever.

[3] Earning per share.
[4] Net Asset Value.

A few days after I joined BABYLON I was passing by his cabin when I saw a posse of people pour out from it. As they trooped out I heard Abel call out after them.

"And listen guys, you must remember that we are located in a high seismic zone . . . an earthquake is just waiting to happen. So is a fire. . . ." The voice trailed off as the cabin door swung closed.

One of the departing people muttered to another, "Yeah, sure . . . and God can strike us down with bolts of lightening . . . why does Abel always keep fretting and worrying all the time."

The whole episode made no sense to me at that time since I had yet to meet Abel. A couple of days later when we did meet things began to fall into perspective.

Within two minutes of our being introduced to each other he warned me in a low, dark undertone. "Do you know that most road accidents occur due to the fault of others?"

I had thought as much and was about to tell him that when he abruptly begged leave and ran off to stare outside the window at something in the distance. Rather piqued and more than a little curious, I sauntered across and joined him at the window.

"What happened? What are you looking at?"

He pointed a slightly shaking finger at the railway tracks that crossed over a little behind the office building.

"I often wonder what will happen if the train jumps tracks while going past there and hits the office building?"

I gave him a perturbed look as he continued.

"Do you think I should ask Security to include this contingency in the Disaster Management Plan?"

Luckily, Abel did not wait for an answer since I sure as hell had none to give. He mumbled another brief apology and grabbing his cellular phone started calling someone. I took this opportunity to slink away unnoticed.

"What's with Abel? Why is he so jumpy all the time?" I asked one of my colleagues a bit later.

"No one knows for sure . . . but he is becoming increasingly like this . . . the higher he goes up the corporate ladder the jumpier he gets," the man confided. "But let me tell you Abel is decidedly one of the most dedicated guys I have ever seen . . . he is really successful . . . do you know the kind of salary hikes and bonuses he gets?" The man gave it some more thought and added. "I guess a lot of it has to do with the fact that he *is* the keeper of the sheep. It is his job to look after the health and well-being of those who throng the corridors of BABYLON, by taking care of their administrative needs."

"I see what you mean," I nodded in understanding.

"Exactly. Just think about it. How much fun can it be to cater to the administrative needs of several hundred hyper and spaced out individuals? These are people who inhabit Cyberia for the better part of their lives and have little or no clues about interpersonal contacts."

"Quite," I concurred. "Even as a kid I remember my nanny telling me never to become a cyber nerd. She always warned us that for these guys, intelligent conversation meant inputing alphanumeric stuff into their computers or clicking icons with their mice/mouses whatever.

"The majority of them think dating means sending off-line messages and foreplay comprises chatting on the yahoo messenger." The man was getting positively enthused by now. "Do you know that most of them think the ultimate Alpha male is one who could discuss Hyper Threading Technology?" He made an exasperated sound. "So sorry is their lot that they even use online reminders to remind them of the birthdays and anniversaries of their families."

We were about to expand on this theme when we saw Boss walking towards us and broke off and headed for our cabins.

Consequently, Abel, though an able-bodied man, was kept seriously busy as he struggled to keep the entire machinery running smoothly and perennially soothe frayed nerves, ruffled egos and raging tempers. Since administration, being what it is, can never run without hitches and problems, a major part of his job entailed trying to keep the flock at BABYLON calm.

As far as Abel was concerned, even when things seemed to be going perfectly all right disaster lurked on the fringes, just waiting to leap out and get at him the minute he lowered his guard.

I remember once when we all pulled up into the office car park in the company minibus that used to ferry us. Abel came rushing out. "Thank God you guys have reached safely. I was so worried."

"Why? Why were you worried Abel? Has something happened that we should know about? Has there been another terrorist strike in the city?" One amongst us queried.

"No . . . no . . . nothing of that sort has happened. Not that I am aware off . . . not that I'd be in the least bit surprised if it did," Abel replied in a most preoccupied manner, wringing his hands, "it's just that one never knows which vehicle can meet with an accident. Or something . . . you know how it is . . . life is so full of dark, unpredictable things just waiting to happen."

"That's true, Abel," the inquisitor replied gently, "but if these dark things are unpredictable then we cannot really do much about them. Can we now? And if that is true then why worry about them?" Then seeing the look of frantic worry on his face, "There . . . there . . . it's all right, Abel . . . why don't you stop fretting and relax a bit. Why don't you let Francis of Assisi guide you?"

"Francis of Assisi? Never heard of him. . . ."

"I didn't think you had Abel. He wrote what we call the serenity prayer—*Dear God, grant me the serenity to accept things, the things I cannot change, the courage to change the things I can and the wisdom to know the difference.*"

Abel pondered over this for a moment.

"Yeah," he replied, "but Francis of Assisi didn't have to worry about sharing the roads with these call-centre cabs . . . or the Corporation bus drivers. Have you seen how devastating. . . ."

"Oh all right, Abel . . . relax, will you . . .?"

"You're right," replied Abel, looking not in the least reassured. "I will . . . I will relax . . . soon as the last three vehicles have come in." Then he wandered off in a most desolate fashion, mumbling darkly to himself all the while.

The result of Abel's worrying nature was that he was decidedly the busiest and most troubled guy I have ever come across. He was always dealing with some real or potential problem, no matter when or where you met him. Many a time I saw him emerge from the restroom mopping his brow, or stand in the seventh floor balcony staring moodily at the concrete below as he clutched a cigarette in his trembling fingers. I quite felt the burden of the cross he was carrying and used to feel sorry for him. But the day I really got worried about him (and ran to the HR Director to tell him so) was when I was passing by his cabin and saw his screensaver. This is what the slowly revolving words said—

Quis Custodiet Ipsos Custodes

In relentless litany the words scrolled across the glowing screen. I could imagine Abel staring at them with dull eyes as he stood like Ruth amidst alien corn.

Now, my knowledge of Latin is restricted to the porcine variety and I am no authority on Decimus Junius Juvenalis, neither have I given much thought to his Satires. Even so, this much of Latin was well within my mental faculties.

'Who (indeed) will guard the guards?'

Thinking of Abel maintaining a relentless and lonely vigil over this frantic, perennially crumbling fort under an endless siege made my heart bleed for him. I could feel his solitude and despair as everyone unloaded on him and he worried about every possible thing that could go wrong. All the while he had nary a shoulder to turn to. I have but a very cursory acquaintance with Jung and Freud, but I immediately realised that the screensaver was Abel's muted and wordless cry for help.

"I think we should get him to a shrink, Headman," I said to the Director HR. "Fast! Before he goes into convulsions, or hysterics, or whatever."

"Don't worry son, I have known Abel for well-nigh fourteen moons and 'tis indeed a strong man that he is. Are you not aware of the amazing manner in which he has succeeded and risen up the corporate ladder? He started life at the bottom of the food chain and see where he has reached now. Don't worry, Model. Let me have a talk with Abel and see what needs to be done . . . we will take it from there."

"Are you sure, Headman?" I asked dubiously.

"Yes, of course. I know Abel well."

I walked away, not very reassured, but feeling helpless before the Headman's implacable reply. My heart was deeply troubled by Abel's plight. I was even more troubled as I passed by the window overlooking the balcony and saw Abel standing there yet again.

The smoke from yet another meaningless cigarette curled away in the wind as he stared moodily at the concrete below. I wondered what dark thoughts were haunting his mind.

In fact, that night, several times I was startled awake with a scream as the dull thud of Abel's body hitting the concrete (as it hurtled down from the seventh floor) shattered my sleep. I caught scarcely a few winks that night.

The next morning I was very relieved to see Abel walk up to his desk, even though he looked tired and fevered, as though the burden of the cross he was carrying was becoming too heavy for him. A sense of foreboding hung darkly over my mood that morn.

Maybe that is why I was not in the least bit surprised when a loud scream rent through the hustle and bustle of the office. As I dropped my post-lunch coffee and hurried forward, I heard the scream again. This time the words were clearly distinguishable.

"Abel has fallen! Brave Abel has fallen! Someone call an ambulance. Please hurry, he is sinking fast."

"Didn't I tell you so?' I threw a hard look at the Director HR as we all raced towards the place where the screams were emanating from. I came upon a sight so ghastly that it jolted me to the very core. Never in my years in the Corporate Jungle had I seen a sight so blood-curdling.

An ashen-faced Abel lay on the floor; his head cradled in the lap of the boss's secretary as she frantically fanned him with her access control card.

"Sprinkle some water on his face." She screamed at no one in particular. "And one of you loosen his belt and take off his shoes."

Two enthusiasts rushed forward. One began to rain water on him while the other relieved him of his shoes.

"What is that terrible smell?" Someone fearfully asked as a strange deathlike smell swept through the corridor throwing the fear of God into all of us.

"I think Abel's socks are reacting with the fresh air…," choked the poor sod who had removed the shoes as he fell back gasping and gagging.

I retreated a few steps to give more room to the fallen Abel and because the stench was too ugly to bear. Somewhere deep inside me I knew this was the last we were going to see of Abel. In fact most of us gathered around seemed to think so too. This was evident from the terror-stricken *Oh-My-God* look that played footsy with the *Thank-God-It's-Not-Me* look on the pale faces gathered around.

We were waiting for the ambulance to arrive when all at once there was an excited hiss and a pulse of excitement ran through the crowd. Instinctively we all edged forward, morbid curiosity getting the better of us.

I felt a cold shudder run through me at the sight that fell upon my eyes. Like something out of a Stephen King novel, I saw Abel arise slowly. Trembling and swaying, he stood gray and ashen-faced in the flickering neon lights of the corridor. A tottering Abel finally stood almost erect, supporting himself against the corridor walls. He gulped down the water that someone handed over to him and then proffered a weak, apologetic smile to all of us.

"Sorry, folks, for all the fuss I have caused."

There was a *come on Abel it's alright* murmur from the gathered multitude. Then a hush fell upon us as we all waited him to go on, although the few less couth amongst us gathered there that fateful day said, "*What happened, Abel?*"

"Oh, it has been a tragedy of errors," said Abel in a weak whisper. "You see I missed my lunch today, in fact I haven't managed to have lunch or dinner the whole of this month . . . I have been so busy that I just didn't get the time . . . there have been so many things happening and so much that could have gone wrong. Somehow something or other always seems to come up just when I'm about to go for a meal . . . oh, oh . . ." Abel broke off gasping for breath and clutching his head he fell to the floor again, to the accompaniment of a delirious "Oh, Oh!" that went up from the crowd.

"Stand back . . . stand back . . ," yelled an energetic-looking security guard as he launched into an energetic CPR while the Boss's secretary went back to her frantic fanning routine.

Abel gasped his last just moments before the ambulance pulled into the portico and paramedics rushed in to aid and succour him. They were scant seconds late, since the ambulance had gotten stuck in one of those perennial traffic jams that plague urban life these days. One of the many things Abel had always worried about had finally come true and that too at a most unfortunate time for him. It was a solemn and depressed lot that stood around as the paramedics tried to revive Abel in vain.

Shortly thereafter the police arrived. Soon all that remained at BABYLON to remind us of Abel was his outline marked in chalk on the floor where he had fallen; a stark reminder of those who spend their lives worrying about things they have no control over.

A little later we all dispersed mournfully. The powers that be at BABYLON decided to call it a day and in memory of the fallen corporate warrior they even lowered the company flag fluttering weakly outside the office building to half-mast.

Feeling low and confused, I packed up my laptop and decided to go home to continue my musings and discuss the whole thing with my friends, acquaintances and other worldly-wise people.

Whilst waiting for the elevator to take me down to the basement parking lot I overheard this really plump lady telling another equally well-fed one, "I fail to understand how Abel could have done such a dumb thing to himself. How could he ignore such basic and essential needs just because he couldn't stop worrying about all kinds of things that could happen?"

The other one also jumped into the fray with equal vigour.

"Why dost thou talk only about Abel, Nora? Can you not see how many of us do the same? We allow the uncertainties of the future to mar our present. Yes, *we must plan for the future, but we have to live in and enjoy the present.*"

They continued in the same vein as we waited for the elevator. When it finally arrived I realised that I just couldn't bear to enter it with them. The thought of being in an elevator with such massive heavy weights petrified me. I was not sure if the cables would be able to bear their collective weight. Otherwise I would surely have jumped in to hear more, for their words had given me the clue to the Lord's Fifth Commandment—

Thou Shalt not Worry about Things Ye Cannot Control

The more I pondered over this and discussed it with my friends and well-wishers, the more I realised the depth of wisdom that it contained and how hugely it could contribute to living life happily.

Having given it another couple of weeks to ensure there was nothing else that I was missing out on this phase of my mission, I came to the conclusion that my purpose at BABYLON had been served.

Even otherwise, I often found myself at loggerheads with those who managed and directed things at BABYLON. More than anything else, it was the extremely poor quality of food at Babylon that became a bone of contention between the management and me. It led to much bickering between us. Finally after we had both seriously chewed the fat, we decided to part ways and that too with a not very pleasant taste in the mouth.

- *One must think and plan for the future, but not allow worries about future problems to blight our present.*

- *Fools prefer to learn from their own mistakes and experiences.*

- *Success is irrelevant if we are unable to realise it and enjoy what life brings our way.*

- *We must learn to accept that which we cannot change and that over which we have no control.*

Thus spake Model . . .

Month Nineteen and Day Three P.D.A.

Thus spake Model . . .

As usual the lady from the Lord's consulting firm had called me within hours of my not-so-glorious exit from BABYLON.

"You quit BABYLON because of the quality of food?" she asked incredulously.

When I murmured in the affirmative, as I did not wish to tell her any more than that, she ranted on, "Good Lord! I cannot believe that any one would leave a job just because of food. What have things come to? Does man live for bread alone?"

I let her blow off some more steam before I gently reminded her that I was still holding on for her. She gave a final exasperated sigh and then said, "You must report for an interview at 09:00 hours tomorrow, on the third floor of the building overlooking the third hole of the golf course. This is a company called WIND, WIND, WIND & WHIRLWIND."

Pause.

"Did you get that?"

"Yes ma'am, I got that."

"Very well. Please be sure to put down your food choice in your resume. I sincerely hope the food there appeals to your exalted palate and is light on cholesterol," she said in a tone heavy with sarcasm. "I suggest you make a good impression by being there on time. Please synchronise your watch now. When I say time, the time will be 10:22 hours . . . TIME."

Having done that she wasted no time in hanging up on me.

I really didn't allow her anger to bother me overly. In any case, by now I was rather sick of treading the beaten track and working with BPOs, IPOs, dotcoms and routine stuff like that. I was dying for a change of scene. Consequently, I was pretty bucked when the Lord's learning curve delivered me to the shores of a firm dealing with the non-conventional.

The next day, bang on the stipulated time, I reported for my interview. I found no one there except some housekeeping personnel who were putting the finishing touches to the cleaning and mopping up.

Upon being queried, one of them magnanimously replied, "It is almost time, sir. Soon everyone will be here."

"What time does the office start functioning?" I asked him.

He gave me a strange look and ambled off with a murmured "soon."

I decided to utilise the time of the waiting by going through the various magazines that adorned the Reception area. Most of these magazines related to the company. I am sure this was time well spent because I managed to go through all the magazines and was pretty much clued in about the company when the Director HR finally interviewed me at about 13:00 hours.

"I am so impressed and thrilled that you know so much about our industry and our company," he said to me barely ten minutes into the interview. "It would be a pleasure to have you on board WIND."

"The pleasure would be mutual," I replied.

"Say, in that case, why don't you sign up here and get cracking . . . post haste. Why waste any more time with all this nonsense?"

I was thrilled to learn that they loved me so much. In any case, I myself was in no mood to waste any time and agreed forthwith.

Consequently the coming Monday, barely a few hours after the crack of dawn, saw me swinging my way into WIND dressed up in my Sunday best, dripping with positive attitude and a brand new Day Timer clutched in my hand.

"WIND, WIND, WIND & WHIRLWIND INCORPORATED is one of the world's largest corporations dealing in alternate and non-conventional energy sources." The public relations person who had been detailed to brief me about the company said to me, when she finally found time to meet me that evening.

"We all affectionately call it WIND . . . even though, strictly speaking, that is not completely correct since WIND is also into solar and other non-conventional energy sources. In fact I would have you know that our windmill is made of cutting-edge SWERVE technology. Our mills stand out in the plethora of run-of-the-mill windmills that are flooding the market. They have been instrumental in making WIND the undisputed market leader." "In fact WIND's backward integration is yet another area of serious excellence and undisputed market leadership," she continued as she led me through the workplace. She literally puffed up with pride as she spoke.

"That . . ." she pointed at the large corner office, "is the office of Mr Spock, our CEO. He is a really dynamic man who has promised that he would deliver all of us to great heights."

It didn't take me long to realise that he would have done it too, if he had been able to find the time for it. Mr Spock' favourite saying was,

If it's not been done before, let's try it. . . . It may work!

Well most of the time it didn't, but who was to tell him that most of his ideas were just a lot of hot air. In any case, often the journey proved to be rather memorable, if not fruitful. He was also very fond of saying things like, *let's wrap this up tonight people*; *guys, this needed to be done last week*; *time is of the essence*; and *darn, why are there only 24 hours in a day?*

Not only did I find this to be a diverse and different role for me, I was pretty sure that my tenure at WIND would be a change of scene and a welcome breath of fresh air. I was not far off the mark in thinking along these lines, since the very first day showed me just how unconventional WIND was.

"You will need to meet Boss tomorrow before getting down to the daily toil," the lady told me when we parted ways at the end of my tour.

Consequently, the next morning I walked into Boss's office at the duly appointed time. I was a bit surprised to see almost half a dozen people hanging around in the waiting room. A harried-looking lady hurried up to me.

"Hi! I'm Harriet. The Boss's executive assistant. You must be Model." She shook hands with me. "Welcome to WIND. I am so sorry, but you are going to have to wait a while. The Boss's first meeting overran and things are a bit behind schedule." She gave me an apologetic smile.

"That's fine Harriet," I motioned towards the waiting masses. "I guess I'll just join the queue." She hurried off after ensuring that I had a cup of coffee and a magazine to pass the time gainfully.

The coffee and the magazine were soon confined to the dustbin of history, yet the length of the queue had not diminished perceptibly. I spent a few more moments trying to catch up with some games on my mobile phone, but gave up as the incessant snoring of the guy in the armchair next to mine really got my goat.

He would snap out of it every few minutes, give an apologetic smile all around and mutter, "Sorry, sorry. I travelled from the other end of town for this meeting. In fact I got up really early to beat the traffic and reach here in time for the meeting and have been waiting for almost two hours now. I'm really very tired and fed up, you see. . . . Very sorry." Then, a moment later he would again slide into a stupor and resume snoring.

Much as it annoyed me, I could appreciate his plight and sympathised with him. More than once I advised Harriet to check with the Boss if I should return later.

"Please give me a moment to check, Model," Harriet would reply as she hurried off. Many moments would pass by, but Harriet never got back with a reply.

Oh well!

To cut a long story short, the pre-lunch hunger pangs had long subsided when I finally got my five minutes of fame with the Boss.

"Model, my dear fellow, so good to have you on board." Boss bustled to the door and greeted me with a hearty handshake as I entered his office. "And damn sorry you had to wait, but I have really been rushed for time today. What to do?" He shrugged helplessly. "I know time is of the essence . . . but there is so little of it . . . anyway, what I wanted to meet you about was. . . ."

Just then the phone rang, cutting him off in mid-sentence. Throwing a weird smile at me, Mr Spock spent the next few minutes on the phone.

"I'm really too busy to talk right now," he told the caller. "Could you please call back later . . . yeah about half an hour would be fine."

He put down the phone with a flourish and stabbed the intercom button. "Please hold all calls, Harriet. I do not wish to be disturbed till I am done with Model."

Then he turned to me with yet another magnanimous smile and was about to say something when his mobile phone cheeped. A really tacky caller tune exploded through the office. Mr Spock threw up his hands heavenwards and grabbed the phone. I sat through another fifteen minutes as he patiently explained to his stockbroker which stocks to buy and which ones to sell, pausing once in a while to flip through his diary and cross-check some calculations. Having done that he told the broker he had no time to chitchat with him and hung up the phone.

By now I had mentally given up. I did not register much of the meeting after that. Not only was I about to die of hunger but my mind had shut down for the day from an overdose of caffeine and all kinds of magazines. I had managed to do more reading while waiting for the meeting than I usually did in a week full of Sundays.

I was leaving Boss's lair when a couple of VPs accosted me.

"Hi there, you must be the new Model. Right?"

I nodded.

"Hey! Great meeting you! Come on . . . join us. . . . We are all on our way to the ten o'clock co-coordinating meeting."

"The ten o'clock meeting?" I was a bit nonplussed since my watch showed it was way past lunchtime.

"Yeah, I know," said he, having noted my watchward glance, "we are running a bit late, but what to do. . . ."

Then I was just swept away in the tide and found myself bound meetingwards. We were drifting through the reception area when a really hassled-looking guy accosted one of the VPs walking with us. This guy's shirt had a really cute company logo on his pocket that read—*WE MAKE TIME COUNT.*

"Excuse me, Mr Lateef," said he, "I am from DYNACLOX. We had a meeting scheduled for 11.30 a.m. today. I have been waiting at the reception for over two hours now. I sent in a dozen messages for you." His words came out fast and furious. One could see it was only the fact that he was talking to a major customer that kept him in some kind of control and allowed some modicum of decency to be maintained.

"Oh, dear! Was that you sending those messages?" The VP replied. He did not seem even slightly perturbed by the whole thing. "I'm so sorry, but I have been really tied up today and just lost track of time. In fact, I don't think I have the time to meet with you today. Say, why don't we reschedule for tomorrow?" He started pulling out his diary to check. "Let me see what is a good time for us to meet tomorrow."

More than his words it was his casual, off-hand tone that really added insult to the injury. The poor sap did not even notice that with every word he uttered the DYNACLOX guy's blood pressure was increasing at an alarming rate of one point per word. The explosion, when it came, literally pulverised the poor sap.

"Time! You are checking to see what is a good time for tomorrow? You moron! Do you even have a clue as to what time is all about? Do you realise what it is to waste someone's time by making him wait for hours?"

By this time the excreta was really hitting the fan. There was a sea of red faces all around. By now the DYNACLOX guy was pulling out all stops and one could see several people from amongst those gathered there, silently cheering him on.

"You nitwit! Someone who has no respect for time and no clue how to manage it should not even be hired to sweep floors, let alone hold a senior managerial position. Which idiot made you a VP?"

The hullabaloo attracted the attention of everyone in office and there was a sea of humanity crowding around in the WIND reception area and gawking at the beleaguered VP. Even Mr Spock had emerged from his office and was making his way towards the reception. He came to an abrupt halt at the last verbal volley fired by the DYNACLOX guy. Pausing in mid-stride for a bare fraction of a second, as the implications of the sentence struck home, Mr Spock did an abrupt about-face and retreated to his office in indecent haste.

Having said his piece, the DYNACLOX guy withdrew from the scene with a final, "And you know what? You guys might be big customers, but if you ever need any more clocks, just don't call us, okay? We don't have time for this bullshit!"

The silence that lingered in the wake of his departure persisted long after he had exited. For a very long time no one uttered a word. People hung about in silence for some more time before they finally dispersed to wherever they had emerged from.

The next morning everything seemed to have returned to normal. People went about as though the whole ugly scene had never happened. That unpleasant segment of time seemed to have been erased from WIND's collective memory as though the Official Secrets Act had been invoked.

It didn't take me more than a couple of days at WIND to realise that this casual approach to time seemed to have percolated right down to the lowest rank and file. Everyone at WIND had this lackadaisical attitude towards time. No one seemed to have any concept of time management or the slightest inclination to try and get things done in time.

We all seemed to spend more time in getting things and people together at some vaguely appointed time rather than in getting things done. The result was that nothing ever got done in time and none of us ever reached home in time for anything.

So much so that very soon I was thoroughly disillusioned with WIND. However I rationalised that the Lord knew what he was doing and must have good reasons for sending me here. Keeping this is mind I stopped resenting it all the time and started flowing with the wind.

Another reason why I tolerated WIND despite all this was the presence of Beau and Belle Weather. In the short time that I had been here, I had become rather fond of them. They made the time I spent at WIND quite memorable and enjoyable.

The Weathers were of that strange and rare breed that works all odd hours and takes tremendous pride in what they did and how much of it they did. No matter what time of the day or night you entered office, you would invariably find one of the Weathers present. Whether this was an inherent part of the Weathers' nature or something that the time-*less* WIND climate had bred into them I am not really sure, but the fact is that if ever there was a couple I knew who needed to get a life they were it. However despite this rather masochistic quirk, they were a thoroughly likeable couple.

Beau Weather in his *avatar* as the Administrative Officer of WIND was an extremely efficient guy who made life quite pleasant for all of us. His pleasant, jovial nature made him much liked by all and his toothy smile seriously contributed to the sale of toothpaste amongst WIND's employees.

"This is my wife, Belle Weather," he introduced me to this buxom beauty. "She is the Senior Accounts Assistant at WIND. Let me tell you," he added with a smile, "She is a much sought-after figure since she is the one who looks after employee reimbursements."

Belle worked long and hard to ensure that we, the toiling masses, received our reimbursements within scant weeks of our submitting bills and vouchers. This was an unusual and unexpected trait in one who hails from Accounts and we all, except her Boss, just loved her for it.

"Doesn't she realise she is setting a bad example and a poor precedence for the Accounts Department?" He would tell all and sundry who bothered to listen.

All this notwithstanding, I am quite sure that even otherwise she would have been a much sought-after figure, since she had the most perfect hourglass figure that I had ever set eyes on. Though, in all fairness, her figure had been a bit affected by the fact that she was in a fairly advanced state of pregnancy by the time the Lord's learning curve delivered me WINDwards. Even so it was a sight for sore eyes.

I would give her a big grin whenever we met and ask, "So, how is it going Belle Weather? Is it time? When is the kid due?"

"It goes well, brother," she would reply with a sweet, fulsome smile. "The baby should be along any time now. But since it is a WIND kid, I'm pretty sure it will not be on time."

In fact that is almost exactly what she said to me that fateful day when I passed by her in the corridor. Methinks neither one of us was aware just how portentous the words were. Not knowing what the fates had in store I was equally blasé about the whole thing and replied with a cheery wave, "Be good now and take it easy, Belle Weather. Try and catch a nap or something.

Her "Oh Model! Give me a break! Who has time to nap in office? There is so much to do and no time to do it in," followed me to the door.

Isn't that always true, dear Belle? But are we really doing what we can to respect time and manage it a bit better?—was the unbidden reply that came to my mind. I didn't say it of course as I didn't want to be rude to a lady; especially one who was due to deliver a baby any time now.

The rest of the day just flew by. I barely came to know when lunch came and went, so busy was I, what with all the meetings, conferences, note-taking and delegation of tasks that needed to be done. It was well-nigh 5 o'clock when I was finally able to put my feet up, the phone off the hook and sit back with a cup of coffee.

Barely had I finished the second cup when I heard this huge outcry break out from down the corridor. Rather irritated (at having my moment of leisure so callously destroyed), and a bit alarmed, I came out into the corridor and saw several people rushing towards the Accounts Department. With a growing sense of dread and foreboding I too joined the flowing stream of humanity and soon found myself at the door of the Accounts Department.

At this door the advancing tide ground to a halt because an Amazon-like female Accounts warrior had taken guard, like one of those Spartan guys at Thermopylæ defending the pass against the Persian hordes.

"Halt! None of you can go inside," she said commandingly. Then she motioned to two females amongst us. "You two may proceed. We need some help in there."

When there were a few muttered protests about gender discrimination and WIND being an equal opportunity employer, she raised a hand imperiously. "Sorry, guys, this is going to be an all-woman show. Belle is having a baby."

A medley of thoughts pierced through the shocked silence that fell upon us like a thunderbolt.

Belle was having a baby . . . in office? Good Lord! It was good to have babies, but was it the done thing to have them in office? Not cricket I say! Why couldn't she have her babies at home . . . or the hospital . . . or something?

Such were the thoughts that ran through our heads. No one shared them with me, but I am sure they did, since they sure as shooting ran through mine and you know how simple-minded we males are—we all mostly think alike.

Finally one amongst us spluttered out, "Why . . . how come . . . why is she having babies in office? Why didn't she go to the hospital? Or to her house . . . didn't she know? Or . . ." words finally failed him and he ground to an embarrassed halt.

The Amazon gave him an amazed look. "Of course she knew she was going to have the baby, but the timing went awry. She didn't think it would happen at this time, the poor baby."

The same dumb ass amongst us spoke again. (Some people I tell you, they just never learn. They never know when to stop.) "How did it happen all of a sudden? I thought women could tell when the pains start and stuff. Why couldn't we get her to the hospital in time?"

The Amazon's amazed look now turned to an accusing ("you men kind of") glare, almost withering the dim wit. "The poor baby had been toiling and struggling the whole day with scarcely time to breathe. Just a few minutes back, when she was carting some heavy ledgers to Boss's cabin, her water broke. We called for an ambulance but, before we could say jack, she was on the floor and the baby was on its way."

The extremely informative and illuminating conversation came to an abrupt end as another lady poked her head out from behind the Amazon and said, "Hey! You!" She unwittingly pointed at the dim wit, "Run and get some hot water. You!" She pointed at yet another amongst us who stood there with his mouth hanging open, "Run and get some soap and lots of towels."

When she saw that he was not off the mark fast enough for her liking, she again barked at him.

"There is no time to waste! Don't dawdle. Run! Fetch!"

Then she was gone again, but just for a brief moment.

Time and time again her head would pop out from behind the Amazon standing guard and a stream of instructions would pour out. Or she would come to collect whatever it is that whoever it is had brought as per her orders.

All this time, the rest of us just stood there, mute, helpless spectators, totally overwhelmed by the turn and speed of events.

At about this time Beau Weather joined us. He had lost track of time while on a WIND errand and only just came to know about the imminent arrival of his baby. His face mirrored a seething cauldron of emotions—fear, anxiety, shame, sorrow, joy all fought for supremacy. Like a coalition government each of these emotions survived for a fleeting moment in time, to be rapidly replaced by another. One could tell he was blaming himself for not ensuring that Belle was home and resting at this critical time, or at least having her baby in a hospital instead of the cold, heartless floor of the Accounts office. One could see the remorse and know that he was aware of the suffering that poor time-keeping and management had wreaked upon his dear wife.

Beau was the only one whom the Amazon allowed to stand just outside the door. But the expression on her face made it abundantly clear that she held him fully responsible for the pain and anguish that poor Belle was going through. And of this there seemed to be plenty, judging from the sharp cries and yells that periodically emanated from within the confines of the Accounts Department.

Frantic, feverish and sharp cries of "push! push!" held us all agog. In fact, it seemed as though almost all of us gathered there were involuntarily pushing. One could tell from the foul smell that ran amok in the office.

Suddenly there was a loud inhuman scream from within. Then after an infinitesimal pause another loud yell, followed by a shrill plaintive yelp and then a ululating storm of cheering broke out from the host of females gathered inside. From within, the cry was taken up, "It is a boy! It's a bonny healthy and beautiful boy!"

Even the Amazon's equanimity suffered a brief lull as she involuntarily turned to look inside. A look of pure love broke out across her face and an unwitting whisper escaped her pursed lips, "'Tis a boy! Oh Joy!"

A confused babble of female voices broke out within. Then, suddenly, a Commanding Female Voice cut through the babble, "Look! 'Tis an omen! Look! Like Ghengis Khan was born clutching a clot of blood in his hand, this boy is born at WIND and look . . . he clutches the wind in his tiny hands."

"Where?" "Where?" "Show me!" "Let me also see!" Such cries rent the air within. We all heard and sensed more than saw the commotion inside the Accounts Department. "Move to one side, I can't see anything. . . . Where? Show me! I can't see anything. . . . Since when can you see wind, you idiot . . . you can if you live in Delhi . . . that's not wind, that's pollution . . . look at his tiny hands . . . he is clutching them so tightly . . . let me also see . . . I can't see anything in his hands. . . ."

The same Commanding Female Voice overrode the babble yet again. "O, shut up, all you people."

Silence reigned, except for the baby's gurgling sounds, because he was impervious to the Commanding Female Voice's dictates.

"'Tis an omen, I declare. This wee lad born here at WIND this day holds the wind in his hands. This boy is destined to great things. He shall be a great corporate warrior one day and capture the largest market share known to mankind. Oh Belle Weather! We rejoice

for you! Great shall be thy glory and unmatched his fame! I propose—
let us call him WIND."

"I second the proposal," someone else shouted.

Immediately others took up the cry. Soon the words, "Let's call
him WIND," swept back and forth like a whirlwind. The rising
storm of these words swept all around me as I stood there mulling
over events.

Suddenly my reverie was shattered by a host of blood-spattered
ladies who pushed aside the sentinel Amazon and surged through
the crowd gathered near the doors like a mountain wind sweeping
through the willows. One of them splattered me with blood, as they
swept past headed towards the Ladies Room.

Rather shaken, I withdrew from the door and began to make
my way towards the sanctity of my cabin. As I was easing past the
Ladies Room I heard a gaggle of garbled sentences, moans and
curses issue forth from the door that was slightly ajar.

"What, will these hands ne'er be clean?"

"Damn, my dress is ruined."

"Out, out damned spot."[1]

"I think my time has come. I can feel my pains starting too."

"Don't you dare . . . ."

"Here's the smell of the blood still . . . all the perfumes of
Arabia will not sweeten this little hand. Oh, oh, oh!"[2]

"Oh, if only Belle had not assumed the baby would not be on
time this would never have happened."

"I know," another moaned, "I kept telling her all the time not
to leave it too late."

There were several more such moans and despairing cries, but
my mind had gone into the shutdown mode when the last two

[1,2] Quotes from William Shakespeare's *Macbeth*.

sentences impacted upon it. Running over everything I had seen at WIND so far, I knew without any doubt that the Sixth Commandment could be none other than—

Thou Shalt always Respect Time—Thine and that of Others

I knew beyond doubt that the Lord wanted all of us to realise that the only truly valuable and irreplaceable commodity we have is TIME. Those who do not value or respect time always end up in a mess.

The Lord had sent this message to me so loudly, clearly and repetitively that there could be no doubt about it. Thus, immediately thereafter I handed in my resignation and continued my solitary trek on the divine learning curve.

As a matter of fact I was not the only one who quit WIND. The Weathers were amongst the dozen or so people who were so deeply impacted by the dramatic manner of Wind Weathers' arrival and the message that it drove home and they too resigned. Of course, despite parting ways with WIND, I never did break contact with Beau, Belle and Wind Weathers.

"Just because we are moving on to different jobs, does not mean we should not remain in touch. You know that I look upon Wind Weather in a most paternal manner, as I had been present at his auspicious birth."

"But of course, Model. We must keep in touch." They concurred. "Wind is so fond of you."

"He is a good lad," I said fondly. "I am sure he is destined for great things and I will do everything I can to set him off on the path to glory."

And I did. I remember presenting him *The Ten Best B-Schools* and *Guide to Entering B-Schools* on his first birthday. On his second one I gave him *Count Your Chickens Before They Hatch* and *Business @ Speed of Thought*. Wind literally cut his teeth on profound and moving books like *Leadership Is What Leadership Does*, *Jesus CEO*, *The Art of Positive Thinking*, *I Ate Your Cheese After Eating Mine* and *7 Deadly Habits*.

I was quite thrilled to see that all these efforts were paying off. With the passage of time, Wind grew up into a tall strapping lad. At no time was he ever seen without some stout educational or motivational book in his hand and a pensive look on his face.

That is why it hurt me no end to learn that Wind had deep-sixed his parents' hopes by running off to this remote island and becoming a scuba diving instructor, instead of becoming a person of influence.

Maybe, without realising it then, we had all timed it wrong, put too much pressure on the poor kid before he was ready for it and driven him to it. Maybe all work and no play had dulled his senses and made him do such a senseless thing. I guess we will never know what the real reason for this was, but it was a pretty tragic end after such a promising and prophetic start.

> • *Each one of us has a fixed quota of time available to us during our stay on Planet Earth.*
>
> • *To mismanage time is to waste something that can never be replenished.*
>
> • *There has to be a time for everything and everything must be done in time.*
>
> • *Successful people are those who respect other people's time as much as their own.*

Thus spake Model . . .

M.O.D.E.L.'s *Seventh Commandment*

Month Twenty-Four and Day Seven P.D.A.

Thus spake Model . . .

It was definitely an ill wind that blew along my path at this time, because I came down with a terrific cold and high fever the very day that I left WIND, WIND, WIND and WHIRLWIND.

Even after a miserable week in bed I was barely strong enough to totter to the toilet. The Lord must have been keeping a sharp eye on me, for it was only when the shivers and sniffles had died down that I got a call from the lady at the Lord's consulting firm.

"And why, pray, did you have to resign from WIND?" She asked. I could tell that she was struggling to keep a lid on her temper.

"They have no clue how to manage time," I told her. "I just cannot stand people who don't respect time."

"Well, then why have you been wasting so much of mine?" She retorted rather tartly. When I refused to take the bait and get riled up she resumed. "You need to report to WE-GONE tomorrow if you are keen on getting another job."

It must have been because I was unwell that I was not very upbeat about it initially, but I perked up considerably when she added. "It is a highly respected European pharmaceutical company that has recently set up shop in the country and is looking for fit, smart and enthusiastic people."

Despite my current illness I knew I fit the bill perfectly, so I applied smartly and joined enthusiastically when I got the affirmative nod from them.

I thought this was a rather prophetic placement since not only was I recovering from a bout of illness but, of late, the hernia had been bothering me with ill-timed and acutely uncomfortable twinges. I assumed there could be no better place to get someone to have a look at it than at a pharmaceutical company. I mean, seeing that these guys deal with medicines and stuff.

Consequently, it was not long after I had unpacked my belongings, settled into the cabin allotted to me and paid due homage to the powers that be at WE-GONE that I went off in search of the right (doctor) kind of guy to get some advice on my hernia.

"Where can I find a doctor?" I asked the lady at the reception.

"There is one right around the corner . . . three blocks away," she replied. "Why? If you are unwell I can call for an ambulance."

"No, no, dear lady, nothing of that sort," I assured her. "I mean, which of our esteemed colleagues is a doctor?'

"A doctor?" She seemed puzzled. "None to the best of my knowledge."

"None!" I was confused. "Are you sure?"

"Of course, I'm sure."

"But this is a pharmaceutical company . . . surely there must be doctors here. You know those people who write DR before their name."

"Well, there are none," she replied finally after giving me a long and not-very-pleasant look.

I was walking away when she hailed me. "Wait . . . there is one. A lady called Meena Mehta writes DR before her name. She joined us last week. That . . ." she pointed, "is her cabin."

"Thank you so much dear lady," I said gratefully as I headed for the doctor's cabin. I was almost there when the door opened and an energetic-looking forceful, formidable female popped out. I was a bit taken aback but decided to take the plunge.

"Hi . . . are you Doctor Meena Mehta?"

"Yes, I surely am." She pointed at the nameplate bobbing precariously on her large left breast.

"Hi! I just needed to consult with you for a moment, doctor."

She gave me a long look. I think she liked what she saw, for she happily ushered me into her cabin and motioned me to a seat.

"I'm Model, doctor . . . I have just joined WE-GONE."

"Welcome to WE-GONE, Model." She smiled, studying me with interest. "How can I help you?"

"Thank you doctor," I said. "Well, you see . . . of late the hernia has been troubling me, so I thought I'd take this opportunity to show it to you . . . since that lady at the reception mentioned you were a doctor."

The sharp peal of laughter that suddenly rang out jangled my nerves. I was shocked at her response. Finally she canned it a bit and simmered down.

"Well, Model, I am not that kind of a doctor. I have a doctorate in Pharmaceutical Marketing . . . but I would have no problems looking at your hernia . . . or whatever else you wish to show me."

I blushed. Deep red. Muttering profuse apologies I exited as hastily as I could without being rude. I was darned if I was going to allow her anywhere near my testacies. I'm sure you'll appreciate my viewpoint if you know what these marketing types are like.

I retired to my cabin sadly disillusioned. I had never imagined that these pharmaceutical companies could be so sick. I mean, of the sixty-seven odd employees who worked at the local office, there was not one solitary medical doctor.

I guess All that glitters is not gold.

As a matter of fact, WE-GONE was stuffed to the gills with these really aggressive Marketing types. There were a few Administrative types who added some colour, but the weird, nerdy and sickly looking Accounts types more or less counterbalanced them.

I can tell you, I was thoroughly disillusioned. The only silver lining I discovered later that day as I sat brooding about the whole thing and going through the fine print of my appointment letter was that I was covered to the very maximum for all kinds of medical problems.

I gave the problem due thought and decided it would be prudent to get the hernia treated before I girded my loins and got down to tilling the soil so that I could work with full vigour and zest. In any case I knew beyond doubt that the hernia would give me no peace and not allow me to live up to my potential.

Consequently, giving it a decent gap of a week, I applied for a spot of medical leave to have my hernia operated. And being the enthusiastic and energetic type that I am, I did not just while away my time at the hospital. I spent most of it busily pushing WE-GONE products to all and sundry. No doctor, nurse, medical attendant or employee of that hospital went unsolicited by me. To everyone I painstakingly explained the merits of WE-GONE products and how they went a long way in enhancing the health and well-being of the human race.

There was one occasion when I felt I might have overdone it a bit. That was when I saw one of the doctors about to give a patient an injection.

"My God, what are you doing? Why are you using this DECTON BICKINSON syringe?" I asked, horrified, snatching it from him. "Here take this . . ." I thrust a healthy WE-GONE syringe in his hands.

"Who are you?" He gave me a filthy look. "And how did you get in here?" For some reason he got a mite upset and called in the ward boy to bounce me out of the hospital. He was quite exasperated to learn I was a paying inmate of that esteemed establishment and thus impervious to such .reats.

Such minor setbacks, of course, in no way deterred me. I was busy explaining the merits of WE-GONE products even while I was lying on the operating table waiting for the anesthesia to kick in and send me off to wonderland.

I remember waking up after the operation and asking the doctor peering over me, about to inject me with a painkiller, whether he was using a WE-GONE disposable syringe or not and only then asking how I was doing.

The doctor (it was the same one who had operated on my hernia) gave me a reassuring look. "Of course I am. Look . . . ," said he, holding it up for me, "And don't worry, old chap. Though much is taken much abides and though you are not now that strength that in the old days moved earth and heaven, you shall soon be in heroic temper and singing with the larks."

I do hope I won't be singing soprano.

I didn't say it to him, of course. (Doctors are a strange breed. They need to be constantly assured that you have faith in them.)

Anyway, I knew I had made the right decision when a few days later I returned to work with everything cut down to the right size and all fixtures and fitments working like a top gun.

The powers that be at WE-GONE must have missed me more than I thought since they were pretty kicked to have me back. Almost everyone who was anyone at WE-GONE popped by to look me up.

"Here's hoping that henceforth you will only be visiting the hospital in your professional capacity."

"But of course," I sent them all off with firm assurances ringing in their ears. "You can bet your last pill on that."

I can tell you, in the next three weeks I kicked up quite a storm as I took charge of my department rather firmly. A series of meetings, conferences and presentations enabled me to kick things into place. I soon had everyone assiduously taking notes and dressing up smartly.

I never knew how inspiring my way of working was till one fine day I found the newest summer trainee busily delegating market research work to the housekeeping staff.

"And remember chaps, you must always be dressed up really smartly. That's the only way people will take you seriously when you approach them. And guys . . ." he shook an admonishing finger at them, "do take notes about everything."

I was quite bucked with all the difference I was making to people's lives in general and the work culture of WE-GONE in particular.

It was two weeks later, when I sat back for a cup of refreshing coffee after a hard half day's toil that I again felt the strangely familiar and much dreaded pain in my *derrière*. I was quite surprised since I had not felt this pain for almost a year and I'd assumed I had put it behind me.

A few days later the twinge had increased to a dull yet constant nagging ache. To my horror, by the following Monday it had lost its dullness and had become an awful pain in the butt. It took all my courage to struggle out of bed that fateful Monday morn, but I did. I even drove down to the office and buckled down to the daily toil. Though I seated myself gingerly and made it a point to avoid all sudden movements, I found it impossible to keep that catch out of my voice. Although by mid-afternoon I even managed to camouflage the catch when I realised it was extremely embarrassing clarifying to people why I was behaving as though I had a pain in the wrong place.

In retrospect I realised that if I had understood the gravity of the situation in time I might have gotten the problem under control in no time at all. As things went though, I bore the pain for well-nigh two weeks as I struggled through work, although the pain in my bottom did not really allow me to contribute credibly to the WE-GONE bottom line. Anyway, by late the next week the pain had crossed the boundaries of decency and I again found myself on the steps of another swanky hospital.

"Boss," I said when I called him, after settling down in my well-appointed hospital room, "I am really sorry, but I am going to be away from the trenches for a week or so."

"At this time, Model!" Boss was shocked. "You do know that we have the year closing coming up?"

"Yes, Boss, I know that. I tried to delay it. I really tried, but the piles have become too big . . . just cannot sit on it any longer."

He made a somewhat unpleasant humming sound.

"But don't worry, Boss. You know me . . . I will not waste this opportunity to spread the word about WE-GONE products at this hospital. I have deliberately chosen a different one from the place where I got the hernia cut to size, because I wanted to tap newer pastures."

Despite all this I detected a hint of displeasure and disappointment in his tone. I found this rather callous, but realising that he was merely human and knew not what he was doing I promptly forgave him.

Anyway, to cut a long story short, in the week I spent there I ensured that the doctors, nurses and all thought, talked, dreamt and bought WE-GONE products. All said and done, it was a rather fruitful stay. And, I might add, a successful one too, since I left that jolly old place with all traces of my piles erased and confined to a hazy memory. I put this painful episode behind me and returned to work refreshed and rejuvenated.

This new energy and zest showed in my work. Like a demon I went about restoring all the processes that had lapsed in my brief absence. Within a few days I had restored order and equilibrium to my department.

Till date I have failed to understand why it so happened that my stint with a pharmaceutical company coincided with a veritable rash of aches, pains and ailments. Though I have given the matter much thought, I am still groping for answers. Finally I concluded that this was simply the will of the Lord. He, in his infinite wisdom, had put me on this pain-filled path to ensure I would be really appreciative when the beauty of His Word was revealed to me. I guess it was also God's way of reminding me that without pain there is seldom any gain.

There could have been no other plausible reason why the index finger of my right hand was on the door jamb when my secretary decided to close the door that fateful afternoon. My scream flashed through the corridors of WE-GONE like flood waters in Bihar. The reverberations had barely begun to die down when I spied the top of my finger lying on the floor wreathed in gore and screamed again.

A swift and bloody ambulance ride found me in the lap of the most competent and exotic surgeon that money could buy. I am not sure whether it was the sight of my agony or the ecstasy of not having to put up with my yells, but he administered this huge dose of anesthesia to me (using a WE-GONE syringe, of course; I insisted).

When I eventually came to, this exotic surgeon's equally exotic nurse informed me. "We will have to stitch your finger back on."

Just behind her hovered my distraught secretary wringing her hands in remorse. "Oh sir . . . I am so sorry, sir." She kept crying.

Maybe it was the influence of the anesthesia, but I was feeling full of the quality of mercy and compassion towards my fellow-men (and women, I must add, since I am an equal opportunity person and do not believe in gender discrimination for any reason whatsoever).

"Come here." I beckoned her close. Then with the nurse as witness I assured her I nursed no grudge against her for guillotining my finger. "You job is safe, dear lady . . . as safe as gold in Fort Knox."

Her remorse and tears fled like dewdrops before the rising sun. She was about to saunter off full of smiles when I called her back.

"Do let Boss know that since I am already in hospital I am going to let them have a go at my ulcers also. I may not be effective in the battlefield for another week."

She (for some strange reason) seemed quite bucked about the whole thing. "Don't worry, Boss," she said perkily, "I am sure they will manage to chug along without you for another week or two. You go ahead and get your ulcers sorted out. In fact," she added, pausing at the door, "since you are already in hospital, why don't you have the corns and the ingrowing toenail also sorted out."

I was rather touched by her concern and, I must add, surprised by the commonsense she was showing. Since I was already in hospital it made eminent sense to resolve other pending problems also.

(*Carpe Diem*[1] and all that sort of thing.) This seemed eminently sensible advice, so I called up the doctors and told them to put me in for a complete overhaul, as it were, once they had finished tending to my severed finger.

Within a few hours they had stuck my finger back on and I stopped feeling like Captain Hook. However, the throbbing pain was horrible to bear. Vaguely, through a haze of anesthesia, I heard a doctoral sounding voice say, "My dear fellow, if you want us to take care of the ulcers, the ingrowing toenail and the corn also, you need to sign this indemnity-cum-release."

I thought that was a pretty corny thing to say to a guy who was under the influence. Anyway, realising I had no choice, I extended a shaky hand and affixed my chop to the proffered paper—after diligently checking the fine print and, of course, calling my legal advisor to run through a few dodgy-sounding things.

When I finally came to, I found myself in my room, safely tucked in bed. I had not yet opened my eyes, but I must have shown some signs of life, for I heard one nurse whisper to the other,

"Hush . . . I think I saw him stir. . . . Thank the Lord . . . the poor dear . . . you should have seen the blood from his corns. I thought he would bleed to death."

I opened my eyes and my heart skipped a beat as I saw my reflection in the mirror at the end of the room. There was a sea of bandages with flecks of blood all over my foot and my hand. All I remember was that I raised a despairing hand and moaned, "Oh, who will rid me of this mirror."

Then I must have passed out.

[1] Seize the moment.

When I awoke the mirror was gone, but the damage had been done. That horrible image was indelibly imprinted on my mind. It caused me much anguish and ruined the rest of my stay at the hospital.

However, soon the day came that I was feeling as good as new. I bid farewell to my newfound friends at the hospital and rejoined work at WE-GONE. There was an air of festivity and cheer reigning supreme when I walked into my office that day. There were even a few balloons and streamers hanging hither and thither.

"Hey! What's up guys? What's the occasion?" I asked everyone I came across. All I got in response was sudden silences and sugary smiles.

The first thing I saw when I entered my cabin was a huge GET WELL SOON card on my table. Below the card was a terse note from the powers that be at WE-GONE telling me to be gone, since (they felt) that with these constant hospital trips I was not doing justice to my job. A cheque clearing my dues was clipped to the note. Below that was an invitation for the tea party being held to bid me farewell and to welcome in my successor.

I cannot say that I was thrilled or anything like that. In fact I was rather dismayed at the callous attitude of the WE-GONE management. I was also a trifle sad that I would no longer be able to contribute to the welfare and well-being of the human race. However, my grief was tempered by the fact that my dismissal from WE-GONE implied that the wisdom of the Seventh Commandment lay within my grasp. Also by now, I was convinced that staying on at WE-GONE meant repeated trips to the hospital for something or other.

This thought was lingering on my mind as I chewed upon the lovely chocolate cake at the farewell party. I was taking the seventh bite of the third piece of that delicious cake when, like a flash, the glory of the Lord's Seventh Commandment shone upon me—

Thou Shalt always Take Care of Thy Health So Thou Canst Live a Fruitful Life

Right away I knew I had done the right thing in availing of every possible medical facility while I struggled and toiled for the betterment of mankind in general and WE-GONE in particular. I was happy I was leaving WE-GONE in sound mind and body, with all possible medical problems taken care of.

In fact I realised that it is our beholden duty to take care of ourselves, for only in sound bodies do sound minds lie. If the mind and body are not sound there is little we can do to contribute to the prosperity of the company or the well-being of our fellow men (and women).

Finishing my cake with a much lighter heart, I packed up my belongings and soon I was gone from WE-GONE. Thus, came to an end my stint in the service of the noble medical profession and the good of mankind.

- *Genius, hard work, organised working, dressing well, staying focused, learning from the mistakes of others, working smart and respecting time is all essential, but will not get you anywhere unless you are physically fit enough to get there.*

- *The more you delay in attending to a problem the bigger it will get.*

- *Successful people take care of their health and stay fit so that they can achieve more and enjoy the fruits of their labour.*

Thus spake Model . . .

M.O.D.E.L.'s *Eighth Commandment*

Month Twenty-Nine and Day Five P.D.A.

Thus spake Model . . .

"How are you feeling now?" The lady from the Lord's consulting firm asked me. There was something not very pleasant in her tone. "I hope there are no more health problems that you wish to sort out . . . if there are, please do let me know. I will call you back again later when you are fully healed and ready to do a few strokes of work."

I didn't much like her words or her tone, but I guess one has to put up with all this while walking in the Lord's steps.

"I am quite well, thank you," I replied sarcastically. "When and where do you wish me to report now?"

"Well, should you feel the need for a job and up to doing some work, you may like to meet the people at BUTT . . . and please don't make a hash of it this time . . . I am quite at the end of my tether as far as placing you is concerned."

I took the desired coordinates from her and then made some reassuring noises before hanging up.

It was only when I landed on the shores of BUTT INSURANCE INCORPORATED that I actually began to understand and appreciate just how serious the Lord had been when he had told me that a diverse exposure would be given to me on the divine learning curve. By now, scant were the sectors of commerce that I had not been exposed to.

"You were right, Lord," I confessed to him that night. "No matter where I have gone I had found the wisdom of the Commandments to be inviolate and omnipotent."

He did not reply; but I did not let that deter me and prayed on.

"With every passing day I find myself becoming better and better. My efficiency as a worker and effectiveness as a person is growing in leaps and bounds. Lord, the best thing is that I have to make only a very minor incremental effort, yet the effects are startling."

And I wasn't kidding. I was truly amazed at the huge difference that resulted by just paying attention to such minor and commonsense details. My morale was really high when I clocked in for my new assignment the next morning.

BUTT INSURANCE INCORPORATED was a full service insurance company that liked to be known as "The CYA Specialists".

"*Put your worries behind you*", the company baseline assured all and sundry. "*At BUTT there are no buts about it—in times of crisis we Cover Your Ass*".

Despite being a divine placement, as a newcomer I was confined to parking my car at the outer edge of the BUTT parking lot—a good five minutes walk from the building that housed the cubicle that was my office.

It was my third day at the BUTT office and I was running behind schedule because of a massive traffic jam en route. So, parking my car, I threw caution to the winds and began running towards the office.

I was halfway across the parking lot when a shiny luxury sedan swept around the corner and almost swept me under, for I had dumbly stepped out from between the row of parked cars almost directly in front of it. It screeched to a sharp, nerve-wracking halt inches away from me.

"Hey! Watch out!" The head that popped out of the driver's window froze me right there, with my hands raised in the air. She was not just cute, or beautiful or any such thing. The face was lovely beyond words and glowed with an unbelievable radiance. "Got a death wish, hast thou? I hope you have taken out the BUTT Ultra-Max Triple Rider Insurance Policy."

"Sorry," I raised my hand and gave my most apologetic smile. "I am running rather late, so I was in a bit of a mad rush. And no, I have yet to take out that policy. Good, is it?"

"Oh well, do be careful or else . . . as the neighbourhood wit says, it is better to be Mister Late than Late Mister." She gave a short laugh. "And of course it is. *All* BUTT policies are good. Get one is what I say. Let me park the car and then I'll tell you all about the policy. Don't move. I'll be back in a jiffy."

She gave me another broad smile and yelled with all the unbridled enthusiasm of an insurance agent as she drove off. (Insurance advisor I should say, since, for some reason, they call themselves "advisors" these days. I don't know how politically correct it is, but that is what they insist on.)

I was so mesmerised by her that I forgot all about being late for office and just stood rooted to the spot waiting for her to park. I noticed that she was parked pretty close to the office complex and her slot even had overhead protection.

She must be somebody important . . . someone the company seriously values, I thought to myself, duly impressed.

I smiled my most winning smile at her as she came up to me. Moving forward, I extended my hand and said to her, very suavely I thought.

"Model. The name's Model." I was sounding very cool, but let me be honest: inside I was all shaken and stirred.

Giving yet another stunning smile she shook hands and murmured, "Eve." Her hands were soft and cool. Her touch seared through me like a walk in the rain.

"I am really sorry, Eve . . . didn't mean to give you such a start." Then, by way of an explanation, I added, "I'm new around here, you see."

"Well, well, Model, if you're not careful about the way you wander around you may well be late very soon." The quicksilver smile reappeared. "And I wouldn't worry about giving me a start. Just be sure you don't get a shock. Next time I may not be able to brake fast enough. And if you are a BUTT staffer, then I guess I will not bother telling you about the policy. You will learn about it soon and then sell one to yourself, I am sure." Another smile. "Well, see you around then." She headed for the office.

My last and most memorable view of her was as she paused on the final step to the office doors. She stopped at the huge glass doors and half turned to give me another radiant "see you around" smile. Till this very day whenever I think of her that is how I remember her. With upper torso slightly twisted back, head cocked just so and a lovely smile lingering on her face, from which shone the most mischievous eyes that I had ever set eyes upon. Her jet black, shining hair was being ruffled and tossed by the wind that blew quite sharply. This memory never fails to bring a smile to my heart.

I stood there long after she had gone inside. Her image was indelibly etched on the canvas of my mind. I just stood there rejoicing in the beauty that had passed before mine eyes. From that very moment I just knew, that no matter what happened, I would pursue her relentlessly till a conclusion was reached. Never since Mary had I felt this way for anyone.

By now I was totally enamoured of her and determined to ensure this close encounter actually led somewhere. (Just as long, Dear God, as she was unmarried and unattached. Which looking at the lovely face and exquisite body, I seriously doubted.)

However, I need not have worried too much. I had forgotten that the Lord was in my corner. I had barely cleared my head and entered my cabin when my phone rang. It was the Marketing Director calling me for a meeting. Ten minutes later I was seated in front of him as he briefed me.

"See, Model. We are setting up a team to monitor and evaluate client perceptions and . . . ah, here you are . . ." he broke off and started to rise as the door opened. "Come, come, I was just starting to . . . Model," he turned to me, "please meet Eve, your team leader . . . Eve, this is Model . . . he has joined us recently and so is ideally poised to provide totally fresh feedback."

The smile dancing in her eyes was a sight for sore eyes. "Hullo again, Model."

The Marketing Director seemed a trifle surprised. "Oh! You two know each other . . . good, good."

"We kind off ran into each other just a few minutes ago," Eve clarified with an impish grin. "Had I been a little slower in braking my car this meeting would have been *about* him and not with him."

The rest of the briefing passed by in a haze. I didn't take much notice of anything that was said, since I was totally engrossed in eyeing her from the corner of my eye and mentally drooling over her. Luckily I did not have to bother about listening to what was being said since, by now, taking notes had become second nature to me. I could literally write with my mind closed. Even otherwise, my backup, the old trusty Dictaphone was silently whirring away, faithfully recording every word for posterity. So I knew I could always run through the meeting whenever I wished to.

Consequently I spent the whole time just feasting on Eve with my eyes. Of course, every once in a while I closed my eyes and mentally kneeling before the Lord kissed His hand and shot off a silent prayer heavenwards for this good fortune.

Thank you, my Lord, for bringing her into my life and for making her the leader of our two-man (sorry, two-person) team. Thank you, Lord.

The next three weeks passed by in a divine haze. I remember nothing about them except that I got to spend ten hours a day with her: just gazing at her, watching her smile, observing her lips as they pouted just so when she was thinking, her breasts move as she did, and . . . and . . . Oh! I must shamelessly admit I spent those weeks looking at her, adoring her, lusting for her and coveting her.

Not for one moment did I think that my passion was unrequited.

A week of stolen glances later, we exchanged our first meaningful and heart-to-heart look when we met one evening at the first birthday of the Manager Production's third child.

The very next day we met again outside the central conference hall. We had all gathered there to attend the departmental inquiry into the sexual harassment allegations made by Delilah, Executive Assistant to the Director, Fixed Assets, against him. While shaking hands we held on for a touch longer than necessary.

We exchanged long, passionate looks when we met the next day at the staff conference addressed by the Director, Fixed Assets, to confirm that all issues and misunderstandings between him and his assistant had been laid to rest. Though we were seated at opposite ends of the room, that was when we started looking into each other's eyes.

I barely heard the Director Fixed Assets say, "I was merely trying to squash an errant mosquito when I allegedly slapped Delilah's behind. There was nothing else too it . . . really."

I barely noted the earnest look he bestowed upon all of us as he added. "It was a very big mosquito . . . I was afraid it would do her great bodily harm."

Eve and I were still looking at each other when he painstakingly began to explain. "And let me tell you folks, when I asked her to take the place of my laptop, I was merely asking her to be more efficient . . . unfortunately she misinterpreted my words and assumed something else. . . . Honestly . . . I have nothing but the greatest respect and admiration for Delilah . . . she is a lady with tremendous assets."

We were still visually locked when he concluded by stating that "despite all this, just to avoid any possible stigma for the company, I am resigning with immediate effect. After all, the welfare of the company comes first . . . always and every time."

He gave us all yet another deeply earnest look as he stepped off the podium. I thought he appeared a trifle sad that his words met with no applause.

We were still looking at each other when Delilah, the buxom Executive Assistant, came onto the podium.

"It is possible that I may have misunderstood things completely." She went on to explain that she might have erroneously been making mountains out of molehills. "I have been deeply touched by the boss . . . no, no . . . I don't mean *that* . . ." she gulped nervously, "I mean his gesture to resign, and I am planning to follow suit to avoid any kind of embarrassment to the company."

Thereafter the gathering broke up. I did take a few moments to look away from Eve when I went to chat with the soon-to-be-ex-Director, Fixed Assets. All my morbid curiosities were seriously aroused by this episode, especially since the office grapevine reported that his wife was leaving him because of this and several other such escapades in the past. I just could not figure out why someone would jeopardise his hearth and home for eleven minutes of physical gratification.

Consequently, despite the fact that I hardly knew him, I found myself asking, "Why, brother? Why did you get into this? Why mess up your home for so momentary a pleasure?"

He did not take my curiosity amiss. In fact, in some strange way, he seemed eager to talk about it. I guess it was one of those guy-to-guy things. Also, maybe, he needed to unload to someone who was new on the scene and could see things objectively and non-judgementally.

"That, my dear Model, is a profound and perennially recurring question. I don't really know if anyone ever knows why we stray from the marital bed. Adultery, bigamy, polygamy . . . or even poly-andry for that matter—they are all such confusing issues, more so when it is the man who has strayed. I mean just look at history . . . Arjun . . . Heimdall . . . people look askance at them . . . especially these feminist types . . . yet, can you believe, they consider Draupadi the victim . . . oh well."

He shrugged as his voice trailed off into a long, thoughtful pause. He gazed at some distant point in space for some moments before he resumed.

"I don't really know why I did what I did. Maybe it was just the monotony of monogamy . . . may be a sense of dissatisfaction and frustration that got to me. I really don't know. You see, my wife is fat . . . *really* fat. Living with her I used to feel like a bigamist even when I was as pure as driven snow. Anyway, all that is. . . ."

He then wandered off with a vague gesture as though he had suddenly run out of words or he thought that whatever he had said was explanation enough. I mulled over his words of wisdom. Then realising that they did not leave me much wiser, I went back to gazing adoringly at Eve.

We were still busy looking at each other a few days later when we met at the farewell tea party that was hosted to bid adieu to the Manager Procurements. A highly intelligent and scientifically inclined bloke, he was being relieved of his duties since he had taken the theory of relativity too far and been busily accepting the bids of one of his relatives to supply furniture items to BUTT INSURANCE INCORPORATED, even though they were not the most competitive bids.

I don't know how many people in the office noticed Eve and me interacting or what conclusions they drew. The first I realised that we were being considered an item was when, one day, during the lunch recess, as I was walking down the corridor towards the canteen, a hand reached out and pulled me into this small dark alcove.

I was about to scream with alarm when the intruder hissed out in a fervent whisper, "Sshhh, don't make a sound for I come in peace. I mean no harm. I am not here to bury thee, but to warn thee." He waited for me to calm down a bit then continued, rather accusingly I thought, "What art thou doing with her?"

"Her? Who's her?" I asked. "What on earth are you talking about?"

"Fie, fie!" He gave an exasperated cluck. "Dost thou think we all are blind? We all know what is going on. Why art thee carrying on behind her like a love-sick puppy?"

"Excuse me?" I retorted, becoming dignity personified. These canine comparisons were quite getting my goat.

"Listen," his tone was really curt now, "I don't have time for thy self-righteous bullshit. What art thou doing with Eve? Do you know who she is?"

"Yes, of course I know who she is," I replied sarcastically. "She is the VP Marketing."

"You idiot, I don't mean that. Hast thou lost it? Dost thou know whose daughter she is?"

"Daughter? No I don't? How should I know whose daughter she is? And what's that got to do with me?"

Another exasperated hiss erupted from him. "She is HIS daughter?"

"His?. . . who's that?" By now I was totally confused and exasperated.

"*HIS!*" He hissed frantically. "She is HIS daughter . . . *He Who Must Not Be Named.*" He suddenly started, his voice dropping to a harsh, strident whisper. "Beware, Model, beware the Ides of March. The last one who dared to transgress had his promotion stalled. And no, this was not the end of his travails. Why, they even turned down the air conditioning of his cabin and blocked his msn messenger."

A cold finger of fear slithered down my spine as the horror of these draconian measures swept through me. "No!" A horror-struck whisper escaped me. "They blocked his msn messenger?" I gasped. I was about to query my unknown benefactor further, but he eluded my grasp.

As he began to dart away he hissed a final, terse warning. "Beware Model. *Beware of that particular tree.* And remember, thou shalt not eat of it: for in the day that thou eatest thereof thou shalt surely die."

Then he was gone, melting away in the intermittently neon-lit corridor, leaving me standing there with a mixed bag of emotions and confusion in my mind.

Whose daughter was she? And why did I need to beware of him, whoever he was? Who was he? Why was he (the man who had accosted me) so scared of him that he was not even ready to name Eve's father?

Shaking my head and resolving to clear up this mystery post haste, I shrugged off the feeling of foreboding that had befallen me and strode back towards the main office area. I headed straight towards the cubicle of this guy with whom I had struck up a hi-how-are-you-doing kind of relationship. We had even shared a beer together one weekend.

Pushing open his cubicle door without bothering to knock, I asked (a bit louder than normal, as my heart was still racing from the close encounter in the corridor), "Hey, bud, who is this guy . . . He Who Must Not Be Named?"

This guy had been sitting with his back to the cubicle door when I spoke. He started violently. There was a loud crash as the optical mouse slipped from his suddenly nerveless fingers. The LCD monitor flickered wildly and his spaceship got shot down by a swarm of marauding aliens as his attention wavered from the computer game he had been playing. His face went totally white, so much so that for a moment I thought he was going into cardiac arrest.

"Hey! Are you okay?" I asked anxiously.

He leapt out of his chair with frantic energy and catching my arm, pulled me inside the cubicle, after a quick look around to ensure no one had seen or heard me. Then he turned to me, his voice hoarse with fear, "Shit! Art thou nuts? You must not say such things loudly. Don't you know who he is . . . He Who Must Not Be Named?"

"No, I don't. That is why I am asking you, dammit! Who is he? And why is everyone so scared that they don't even want to take his name?"

He again darted out and peered out of his cubicle, looking both ways to ensure the coast was clear. Then coming close to me, he leaned forward till he was almost in my ear and spoke in the smallest whisper I have ever heard. "*Boss!*" Then, seeing my bewildered look, he hissed again. "No, not Hugo Boss, you moron. *The* Boss." Saying so he pushed me out of his cubicle. "Now go, Model. Embrace this occasion to depart." He pushed again, harder. "And stay departed for God's sake. Just stay the hell away from me?"

That's the last time he ever exchanged a civil glance with me. Thereafter, whenever our paths crossed, he either looked through me or in the other direction.

I spent the rest of the day in a bit of haze, with a medley of tumultuous emotions seeping through me. All at once I became keenly aware of the looks that my co-workers were giving me. All my interactions with them seemed so contrived. Everyone behaved as though I had bird flu. All at once I felt alone and isolated. Even Eve did not come in for work that morning, so I had no one to talk things over with. Somehow I stumbled through the day, depressed and dejected.

My moodiness and confusion must have been clearly manifest when I met her the next morning. Within a few moments she noticed that I was behaving a bit off-key. She just looked at me and said, "So, you know." There was a world of sadness emanating from her. "So, now you too would like to walk at least a few feet away from me."

I thought I could see a faint tear in her exquisite eye as she gave me that *et tu Brute* look that seemed to say, *Go, Model. I set thee free. I have no regrets, grudges or hard feelings. I understand.*

My heart broke as I watched her. After all, it was scarcely her fault that she was His daughter. For a moment the pain caused to me by Mary made me pause. Time stood still as a familiar fear, caution and a sense of *déjà vu* froze me. Then, reminiscent of the English assault on Harfleur, I felt the indomitable spirit of Henry the Fifth sweep through me.

Once more unto the breach, dear friends,[1] I muttered to myself as I reached out, touched her fingers and whispered, "Come Eve, come with me."

We left the office walking about two feet apart, but in a virtual hug and went straight to my apartment. During that drive neither of us exchanged a single word. We just drove with our fingers touching each other lightly.

We had still not exchanged a single word till much after we had known each other and then lay together spent. In fact I don't think either one of us was really in the mood to talk. All I remember of those heady and glorious moments was this extraordinary feeling of lightness in my body and the constant roaring of divine music in my head.

> *Rocks of ages*
> *Clefts for me*
> *Let me hide myself in thee.*

The words echoed in my head in a never-ending litany accompanied by the most divine music as again and again we wildly and passionately knew each other and discovered the wonder of our bodies. Then we spent the rest of the evening lazing in each other's arms and talking of this, that and the other.

The next day.

When I entered office I noticed a sea change in the world around me. There was a clear and present difference and deference in the

---

[1] Quote from William Shakespeare's, *King Henry the Fifth*, Act 3, Scene 1.

way everyone was treating me. Almost as if a notice had been circulated on the company LAN that Eve and me had known each other and were as one.

It didn't bother me. I was too euphoric to care.

Two days later I proposed to her. She accepted.

Two weeks later we got married.

"We will have a small and simple ceremony," Eve's father told us. "Let us just have the three hundred odd employees of the company and about sixty relatives each."

The company picked up most of the tab. (Whatever, I guess it could pass off as staff welfare or business promotion.) It also paid for the lovely bungalow that was hired for the new Senior VP and the new VP Marketing—Eve and me. Likewise, I am sure that the lovely golden paper used to wrap the Stock Options that were presented to us as a wedding gift were also paid for by the company.

The next day we departed for our honeymoon to the Swiss Alps. It was simply divine.

It was on the fourth day after our return that Boss collapsed while walking up to his cabin from the gym. He departed for his heavenly abode shortly thereafter. It was a massive cardiac arrest.

My joy at being father-in-law-less was considerably dampened by the grief that Eve suffered. The two of them had been very close to each other. I stifled my baser emotions and stood by her during these dark hours.

On the fifth day. We stood in silence as his coffin was lowered into the ground. I saw Eve standing on the other side of the grave with a world of grief in her moist eyes and my heart bled for her.

It was on the Seventh Day that The Revelation happened. The new Managing Director called me in. Eve was already there when I entered. A look at their faces and I knew it was an ill wind that was blowing that day. It was. Our careers were about to list. Big time.

"Company policy does not allow spouses to report in to each other. My apologies, but one of you will have to leave."

We both did, the very next day.

I was not unduly worried, since I knew this meant that the Lord had delivered the message that needed to be delivered and my assignment at BUTT INSURANCE INCORPORATED was over.

For a change I did not even have to exercise the gray cells about what the divine message was, for as I was exiting the new Managing Director's office, all of a sudden, from the Lord knows where, these words just echoed through my mind.

It is okay for thee to covet thy Boss, his ass, his wife's, sister's, mother's or daughter's, or your co-worker's, the domestic help's, the client's and/or that of the vendor's that pass through the portals of your work life every day. But thou shalt not under any circumstances, even if they be willing, eager and panting, ever fornicate with thy co-workers, domestic help, clients and vendors. Of special relevance is the fact that thou must never fornicate with your Boss's wife. You must also not fornicate with his sister, daughter or secretary. Not unless you are very certain of your willingness to marry them and of the effect that such a marriage will have on the career path that you have planned for yourself.

The minute these divine words went through my head and I had mulled over them a bit, I realised the Eighth Commandment had to be—

Thou Shalt Always Keep Thy Personal and Professional Lives Apart

It was evident to me that those who mix their personal and professional lives are in dire straits. I was rather amazed that I had never understood such a simple and fundamental thing before.

Happy though I was at having completed the eighth task I was worried to death about Eve. I knew she was deeply troubled by this unfortunate turn of events. So upset was I by her anguish that I threw caution to the winds and fixed up a meet for her with the lady at the Lord's consulting firm when she called me the next morning.

There was grim pleasure writ large on her face and an appointment letter clutched firmly in her hand when Eve returned from the meeting.

"They have asked me to join them as a consultant." There was tight triumph in her tone. "I am going to have so much fun telling people what idiots they are and then making them pay for it."

"I am so happy for you." I gave her a big hug. Inside I was filled with a confused medley of emotions for I knew not what this signified or why the Lord had made this happen. What I did know for a fact was that Eve would not have had to give up a job that she liked so much and start her career afresh if I had maintained my distance.

- *The theory of relativity notwithstanding, it is not prudent to create new relations or to bring your old relations into the workplace.*

- *Successful people do not allow their personal and professional lives to intermingle.*

Thus spake Model . . .

Month Thirty-Two and Day One P.D.A.

Thus spake Model . . .

By now I had become so attuned to the wondrous ways in which His wonders He performed that I knew it was the lady from the Lord's consulting firm the minute the phone rang, just as I entered my house.

"I have something for you," she said tersely. "Go to this website and apply for the job listed on it."

I was quite pleased that the lady was always on the ball with the Lord's work, but I was seriously sick of her impolite attitude. I decided to get to the root of it.

"I'll do that pronto, ma'am? But before you go, pray tell me why art thee always so short with me? Is this how you talk to all your other candidates also?"

"*Candidate*! Is that what you call yourself?" Her voice was literally shaking with anger. "*Sir*! You may like to note that we are *not* some half-assed contingent firm. We are a top tier, retained talent search firm and we have a six-month placement guarantee with all our clients. Do you have any idea how many times in the past few months I have not only had to look stupid because of you, but have also had to provide a free replacement in lieu?"

Such was the anger in her voice that I'm pretty sure if I had been sitting in her presence, she may well have taken a swing at me.

"The Lord alone knows why our Managing Director has taken up your case."

Then why don't you check with the Lord, sis?

That is what I wanted to say to her. I didn't actually say that of course, for one must not take the name of the Lord in vain. In any case, I figured that if the Good Lord had wanted her to know the facts of the case, He would have told her Himself. I decided to be Gandhian and turned the receiver to the other ear.

"Thank you very much for all the efforts you have been making on my behalf," I said politely.

I think she was a trifle mollified, since this time she did not bang the phone down quite so hard.

A couple of hours later, after a quick bath, a hurried nap and an energy-enhancing power breakfast, I powered up my laptop and went to the website that she had told me about. The words of the web page held my attention in totality. I felt a weird premonition kick in, as if I stood on the edge of some monumental discovery.

WELCOME TO
THE PROMISED LAND
REAL ESTATE & DEVELOPMENT COMPANY
~ a name you can trust ~
WE DELIVER

www.ThePromisedLand.com
(Click here to enter)

My fingers moved as though of their own accord and clicked the enter icon even before I realised it. I watched with rapt attention as the next page flickered on to the screen. It seemed to take forever to download, but by now the website had my undivided attention. Yet again I felt a divine hand guiding me onto a preordained path. Another click on the WORK WITH US icon led to this page that said to me;

WE ARE AN EXCEPTIONAL COMPANY
LOOKING FOR EXCEPTIONAL PEOPLE

PEOPLE WITH THE INTEGRITY OF A CAESAR
THE WISDOM OF SOLOMON
THE COURAGE OF ULYSSES
WITH THE DESIRE TO LEAD & TO ACHIEVE
WORTHY OF GHENGIS KHAN

DO YOU HAVE IT IN YOU?

IF you do
please send your resume to Ms D.T.H. Squad, Special
Assistant to Dr G.O. Bells the Managing Director.
We shall revert to you shortly.

If you don't hear from us you probably don't have it in you!
Trust us—we know.

I *knew* I had it in me. In any case, I had been sent here by divine command, so I immediately shot off my resume to Ms D.T.H. Squad. Then I sat back and waited for them to revert. They did revert, within the very next hour in fact.

Please make it convenient to have a power breakfast with our Managing Director, Dr G.O. Bells, at the Radisson Hotel tomorrow morning at nine. Ms D.T.H. Squad e-mailed promptly.

I replied equally promptly.

Please let Dr G.O. Bells know that I shall be there with bells on.

I was pretty bucked by the enthusiasm they were showing, but I guess it was only to be expected since the good Lord must have been showing them the way.

The breakfast went well. Though Dr G.O. Bells didn't come alone. He had a couple of strings attached. (The Director HR and the in-house psychiatrist, I learnt later.)

They grilled me for over an hour. I wanted to tell them to chill out and relax since they would have to hire me in any case or else face the wrath of the Lord, but I was pretty sure the Lord would have looked askance at me if I had done so. So I humoured them along and was so busy answering questions that the fabulous scrambled eggs and toast went cold on me. All in all, divine intervention notwithstanding, I think things went rather well because just a few hours after the meeting I got a call from the Director HR.

"We have given the matter due thought and would be quite pleased if you would like to join us at The Promised Land as Vice President Special Services (VP-SS)."

"I would be delighted," I replied joyously, eager to get on with the Lord's work.

Immediately I detected a slight change in the Director HR's tone and demeanour.

"Of course, the salary can never be commensurate with the real worth of a man as qualified as you are, but you will appreciate that we are currently facing budgetary constraints."

I was about to speak but he just carried right on.

"But then, I guess for an able fellow like you, the real reward is the work and the challenge and not something so mundane as salary… I'm sure you realise that as Head of the SS, you would have pretty much of a free hand and can more or less write your own ticket."

"That is quite true, old chap," I cut in, deciding to cut the bullshit and let the game begin.

The man did not know of the divine quest I was on, or the fact that I was bound by Divine Command to accept all assignments that He sent my way. So he was a mite surprised with the alacrity with which I accepted the offer. In fact, the cheapskate even back-pedalled a bit and tried to renegotiate for better terms. I, of course, put my foot down at this tackiness. Then, not being one to let grass grow under my feet, I reported for duty immediately.

Shortly thereafter I had checked in to my own little cubicle on the eighteenth floor of The Promised Land. It was a really tiny cubicle. So tiny that I got the feeling that if I changed my mind I would find myself in the next cabin. Even so, it *was* in The Promised Land. I felt really good and on top of the world. For once I felt I actually belonged.

The next day I got a call from Ms D.T.H. Squad. "Dr G.O. Bells requests you to join him in his office . . . if you are free."

"Of course, I am free," I assured her. Like most wise men, I am never too busy for Boss. So, after rechecking the tie knot and the shine on my shoes and straightening the trouser crease, off I went to meet Boss, packing my trusty Dictaphone and Day Timer.

Dr G.O. Bells was standing near the large bay window (fitted with one-way glass) that overlooked the gardens and the main parking lot when I entered. His office straddled most of the top floor of the main building so he had a panoramic view of the complete complex.

He seemed lost in deep thought when I entered. He waved a casual hand at me when he noted my presence in a most subconscious way and then went back to his introspection.

I wisely chose not to disturb his reverie. Instead I also joined him near the window and stood looking at the constant stream of people walking from the main office building to other parts of the complex. Unwittingly, my attention was drawn to this really cute and curvaceous lady who had sashayed out of the door and was swaying towards the Admin Block.

I was happily admiring her curves when Dr G.O. Bells murmured softly, "Ah! What an *annus mirabilis*!"

A little surprised at Boss's remark, but going with the flow, I looked even more closely at her delectable *derrière* again before turning to him. "Yes, it is a remarkable ass, isn't it? But Boss, are you sure her name is Mirabilis?—doesn't seem likely for anyone to have a name like that, Boss."

"Eh! What?"

Dr G.O. Bells started as though he had sat down on some sharp, hard object.

"Ass? What ass?"

He then gave a long look at the lady before he turned to give me an even longer look.

"I meant, what a marvelous and eventful year it has been, Model. That's Latin. A-n-n-u-s M-i-r-a-b-i-l-i-s."

He spelt out the words slowly for my benefit.

"Really, Model!" He didn't say it in so many words but his disdainful sniff and pointed gaze did: *If I did want to discuss the asses of the hired help I surely wouldn't do it with the hired help, would I now? You ass!*

Suitably chastened and highly mortified, I stood there feeling like an ass. "Forgive me, Boss, you know that Latin is truly a foreign language for me," I mumbled apologetically.

With a dismissive gesture Boss motioned me towards his table as he moved towards it after one final look at the dancing *derrière*. I could see that he didn't trust me around the windows any longer.

"Model, despite your impressive and varied experience, since this is the first time you have ventured into the real estate business, I want you to start on the ground floor. I want you to mingle with the marketing team as they give their spiel and do their act. I want you to study the lie of the land and learn the ropes before I unleash you to wage a holy war to bring the masses to The Promised Land. Before we cry havoc and let slip the dogs of war it is very important for you to know what the terrain out there is like and be familiar with our basic strategy and tactics."

He waved an airy hand in the far direction as he spoke. Then he went back to some more introspection.

It was a while before I realised that the conversation was over. Waiting for a few more moments just in case Boss needed to say something more, I departed with a faint, "Right then, Boss. I'll get on to it right away."

Keeping in view Boss's views, the next day found me in the front trenches of the marketing office. I was champing at the bit and raring to learn the ropes.

It was a Sunday, so real estate buyers thronged and clustered in droves. Since The Promised Land lay in the shadows of a huge cluster of BPOs, IPOs, IT and ITES units, there was a real mob of young urban professionals all over the place. Though, of course, there was nothing urbane or professional about the way they all vied with and shoved at each other as they all simultaneously tried to get the attention of the Marketing Team to attend to them first. The pushing and shoving just wouldn't stop even though we had several customer relations' executives going around and assuring everybody that there was enough space for everyone in the Promised Land.

I found the atmosphere quite heady and intoxicating. After a couple of reconnaissance rounds of the battlefield I finally homed in on this cubicle where the Marketing Executive was one of these really high-energy types. The pile of signed application forms on his table was the biggest. He, I decided, was the one I would use to further my education about the ground realities of The Promised Land.

With a polite "excuse me" I shoved past this real fat guy and his equally fat wife and squeezed unobtrusively into the corner of the cubicle. The Marketing Executive just gave me a cool nod as I seated myself on the stool in the corner and continued with his sales talk.

"You see, ma'am, it is precisely for the upmarket, elite, sophisticated and discerning customer like you that we have designed these homes." She simpered slightly. "We don't just offer you four walls and a roof over your head. It is a complete lifestyle that goes with it for an exclusive family like yours."

"Lovely," she gushed. "But where is the pool? I do want to teach my children to swim."

"Ma'am, there is a pool table in the cultural complex. As for the swimming pool, we are just trying to address the water problem. Soon as that is resolved we shall plan the swimming pool also."

"But there will be one, right?"

"Oh I am sure there will be one ma'am. See here," he turned to a page on the application form and turned it towards her, "it says very clearly that the charges for the swimming pool, if any, will be extra. Now why would they put in that clause if they hadn't planned for a pool? Of course, nobody will commit to it till they have all the sanctions and approvals." He gave her a winning smile. "You know how it is ma'am."

"Sure . . . sure I quite understand." She was by now totally focused on the application form. She barely noticed herself take the unobtrusively proffered pen from him.

"Talking of pools ma'am . . . did I mention that we plan to encourage all Promised Land residents to start car pools for work and school? Thus we can keep the area less polluted and the streets much safer. After all, the fewer cars we have on the roads the easier they shall be to maintain and the longer they will last. And, of course, the safer they shall be for the children to play on. You will agree ma'am that it is so much better to leave the roads free for the children. We wouldn't want them mucking up the lawns and parks."

She was so busy signing the application forms and he (the husband) was so busy calculating and writing out the cheque that I doubt they heard much. Shortly thereafter they were out of the cabin, happily clutching the allotment letter and munching on the chocolates the Marketing Executive had doled out to them as he congratulated them for the new house they were going to move into in about eighteen months, IF God remained in the Heavens and all went as planned.

Another couple breezed in by the Marketing Executive a few seconds later rapidly replaced them. (These marketing guys were paid on the number of applicants who signed up so they were always in a bit of a rush.)

The Marketing Guy was midway through his selling spiel when the female part of the couple interrupted him. "Why are you making us pay for two car-parking places when we only need one?"

"Good Lord, ma'am, why would you only need one car? You will soon realise ma'am that we have given a lot of thought to the whole project. We have had a bunch of experts from the world over carry out a detailed study of this issue and the profile of the people who are going to live here. You *will* need two cars, ma'am."

"But, why? You have been telling us that everything is so close by and even our workplaces are just around the corner. I'm sure we can manage with one car."

"But what about your kids, ma'am? They are soon going to grow up and need their own car. You wouldn't want them to walk around like mere pedestrians, would you now? We have to be far-sighted and think ahead. That's why, ma'am, two car slots are mandatory and only the third is optional. We are even ready to allot a fourth one should you feel the need at a later date."

Another couple later.

"Of course ma'am, you shall be able to move in at the end of eighteen months. And if you aren't, we shall be only too happy to pay you the penalty mentioned for the delay, unless of course the delay is due to factors beyond our control. See," he pointed to another finely printed clause on the application form, "it says so here very clearly and explicitly."

"Which are the factors beyond your control?" The husband boorishly butted in.

The Marketing Guy gave him a look of sheer amazement, "You know how it is, sir. Almost everything is within our control, except for some things that aren't."

"Yes, that's exactly what I want to know. Which things are not in your control?"

The Marketing Guy barely paused for the duration of a missed heartbeat. "Like rains, sir. You know that it takes longer for the cement to set when it is raining."

"True. But why would you want to put cement when it is raining?—seems a pretty dumb thing to do."

"Ha ha!" The Marketing Guy guffawed long and heartily. So much so that unwittingly and unwillingly the couple also joined in. "We don't, sir, we definitely don't, but you know how these workmen are. Good workmen are so hard to find. That's another problem we are unable to do anything about. Ha ha! You have an amazing sense of humour, sir."

The laughter simply swept everything away. Not long thereafter the couple swept out clutching the appropriate allotment letter and munching the customary chocolates.

The next prospect was accompanied by his wife, mother, father, brother, sister and a child, about three years old. With this wholesome crowd the small cabin was starting to feel like Pandora's box, but it did not seem to discomfit the Marketing Guy at all. In fact, he even involved the kid in his spiel by giving him some toffees and a brochure and asking him to select his bedroom while the adults did more droll things like filling forms, signing documents and cheques. Having engrossed him thus, he turned his full fury on to the Prospect.

The Prospect, after he had listened to the selling spiel for about five minutes, broke in. "What interests me is whether you guys will provide us with the same quality that you show in the sample apartment? Most developers show something when making the sale and then build something totally substandard. That is why I need to be sure that you will give us the same thing. That's all I am interested in."

The Marketing Guy laughed long and heartily. For a moment I thought he had overdone it this time, but eventually smiles started to emerge on the lips of the gathered multitudes.

"That's SOOO well put, sir!" he leaned forward and shook the Prospect's hand admiringly. "You are so right! That's what most of these builders do! But, sir! *Puhlease*! This is The Promised Land! We keep our promises. You can rest assured about that."

The Prospect did not seem particularly reassured. "Yes, yes. That is all very well, but how do I know that The Promised Land keeps its promises? I want you to convince me. That's all I am interested in."

"See, sir, look at this," The Marketing Guy pushed forward the inevitable application form. "Look! Each and everything is clearly mentioned. I tell you sir, we at The Promised Land are very particular about these things. But even so you are right to take such an active interest in this. And talking of interest reminds me sir . . . did I mention to you that we have tied up with the Bank of Babel and Sodom for this whole complex? For the convenience of valued clients like you they will finance 95 per cent of the cost with minimal documentation and at an amazingly low rate of interest."

Thereafter the conversation ebbed and flowed a bit, as they discussed interest rates and how this easy loan would enable the Prospect to buy a five-bedroom apartment and not the smaller one the family had been compromising for.

"I mean, just look at the glorious size of your family," he pointed out. "It is humanly impossible for all of you to live in such a small house."

"But we all don't live together," the Prospect replied.

"That's fine, sir," the Marketing Guy consoled them, astutely pointing out, "but you will keep visiting each other. And when you do those two extra bedrooms will surely come in handy."

Needless to say, the whole brood trooped out a bit later, happily chewing chocolates and clutching the application form. I tell you, the Marketing Guy was like Achilles—really relentless and utterly unstoppable. I sat there and heard him come out with the most ingenious logic and memorable remarks.

The air buzzed with pearls of wisdom like Money is a scarce commodity. A bad workman blames his tools. The floods in Bihar affect the supply of cement in Rajasthan. Drip irrigation is a slow process. It takes nine months to have a baby. There is too much spurious material being sold in the market these days. Delay is an inherent aspect of any project. VAT adds no value to the wallet—the list was endless. And no matter what the situation or circumstances, he always had an excuse or explanation ready.

The more I listened to him communicate with potential clients the more concerned I was about his cavalier attitude, so much so that I decided to counsel him at the first opportune moment. I did not wish to curb his enthusiasm or dampen his spirits but I did think it imperative that he be more transparent and forthright in his selling.

Consequently, when he had successfully clinched yet another deal and before he could move out and usher another couple into the killing zone, I leaned forward and put my hand on his shoulder to draw his attention.

"I must compliment you for your tremendous enthusiasm," I said.

I was about to speak of more serious matters when a sudden commotion and spate of yelling in the reception area made me pause. We both looked up wondering what the hullabaloo was all about when this huge, burly man hove into view. He was breezing past the cabin we were in when he spied the Marketing Guy through the huge glass partition and his face brightened (in recognition) and tightened (with rage). Pushing the cabin doors open he strode in and yelled.

"*You*! It's you! You are the one who sold me the house in May Bach Greens. You told me I would be given possession of the house in January. Well, it is May now and I want my ruddy house or my money back?"

The expression on the Marketing Guy's face made it abundantly clear that he hadn't a clue what the Irate Guy was talking about. (I don't think he saw the faces of the people he sold houses to, just their cheque books. So focused was he on their cheque books that I am even surer that he never remembered what he committed to them.) He, however, seemed to have gotten so used to hazing his way through life that this did not faze him in the least. He did not take long to recover. He spoke out soothingly, slowly and calmly, in a tone that we use for the seriously mentally disturbed or the really irritated wife.

"Sir, please sit down. Here . . . have a glass of water, sir."

The Irate Guy drank the water that was thrust at him.

"Have a chocolate too, sir . . . anger is bad for you and affects the sugar level in the body."

The Marketing Guy smiled winningly and held out a box of chocolates towards the Irate Guy. This apparently innocuous act seemed to throw some switch in the Irate Guy's head. He turned red and his veins started to bulge out. You could see the anger surge again. (I am only guessing, but maybe he was diabetic and didn't relish having things shoved into his face which he wanted to eat, but couldn't.)

Shooting up to his feet again he leaned forward menacingly and yelled. "You sold me the house. You said you would give me possession within twenty months. It is now twenty-four months and I want to know where is the house—*NOW*."

"Please sir, sit down. You must understand that delay is an inherent part of any project. We don't want to have these things happen but they do, sir. To err is human."

This did not seem to impress the Irate Guy much. Waving all this aside he erupted forth again.

"I don't care. I want my house and I want it *now*. I cannot understand why it is taking that long."

"Sir . . . please . . . you must understand, we at The Promised Land never short-change our valued customers. We promised you a house of a certain standard made of materials of a certain specification. Unfortunately sir, the market is flooded with spurious materials and we just cannot give you a house made from them. I'm sure you understand this, sir."

Well he didn't. I don't think he was much in the mood to even want to understand. He just leaned forward and knocked the Marketing Guy down, shouting all sorts of things about compulsive liars, capitalist thieves, communist rascals, Nazi murderers and Fascist thugs.

I saw the Marketing Guy rise shakily to his feet and the Irate Guy knocked him down again. In fact, again and again, as the Marketing Guy tottered to his feet, the Irate Guy knocked him down. I am not too sure exactly what all transpired since I was shocked by the turn of events.

"Security! Security!" I yelled as I hit the panic button installed in the cabin. A loud whooping alarm drowned out all sound. A swarm of storm troopers rushed in and pinned the Irate Guy against the wall. Some semblance of sanity returned. I recovered my wits quickly enough. Knowing that I was the senior most officer of The Promised Land present, I knew it was my duty to handle the situation and cool things down, especially since a whole load of potential customers had gathered around to watch the proceedings with great interest.

"Sir," I said to the Irate Guy, "whatever your grievances, I assure you we shall address them. Please give me the details before you leave. If we have delayed or erred, we shall repay your money and whatever interest is due."

Then, mentally clapping my hands at a job well done, I motioned to the guards to take him out and throw him to the wolves. Reception had already called the police and one could hear the wail of a siren as it drew closer.

Long after the Irate Guy had been consigned to the dustbin of history and the Marketing Guy to the nearby hospital, I was busy brooding over the whole thing when the door to my cabin burst open and Dr G.O. Bells strode in. He was Painful Accusation personified.

"Model, Model, what have you done?" He looked at me shocked and aghast. "Why did you say that to a customer? That too in front of so many other potential customers! Refunding money is against company policy. It speaks of very poor corporate governance and will set such an unwanted precedent."

Rather surprised and taken aback by this I felt the righteous courage of my convictions rise. "Boss!" I blurted out indignantly, "Our marketing guy was going on and on like a used-car salesman, making all sorts of incorrect and inappropriate promises. He was trying to unnecessarily bullshit a client with a very legitimate grievance. What else could I have done? There was no truth in what he was saying."

"*Truth*?" Dr G.O. Bells muttered disbelievingly. "I don't care about all that. As far as our customers go, you have to think hard and fast and come up with some plausible, reasonable-sounding excuse for whatever problem they are facing." He paused for a moment before he mumbled in a disbelieving tone. "The Truth? Forsooth!"

"Yes, Boss. Doesn't he know that the truth is out there? One day it will out and then where will we be? Our reputation is at stake."

Dr G.O. Bells motioned to me, regally, to follow him. He continued when we were out of earshot of the others who had gathered to gawk at us.

"Model, as you go along in life you will realise there is nothing called truth. Truth is but what we perceive of it. What is true for you may be totally irrelevant and untrue for me. So don't give me that jive, Model. Tell me, do you have any excuse whatsoever for your totally unexpected and uncalled-for behaviour."

Righteous anger at the sheer unfairness of it all overcame me. No matter how accustomed I had become to the persecution that was wreaked upon those who follow in the wake of the Lord, I can tell you that I was feeling pretty cut up right now. All told, although my year was going wonderfully, right now it surely was not going well at all. I just could not help blurting out.

"But, Boss, do I need an excuse at all? I think I did the only possible thing under the circumstances. We, at The Promised Land, need to be careful about what we promise, and then ensure that we deliver on our promises. *Satyamev jayate*,[1] Boss, *satyamev jayate*. In the end the Truth always wins."

"I have no clue what wins in the end, my friend, but I doubt we will be around when it comes, so let's not worry too much about it," Dr G.O. Bells intoned. "You must always remember that in business there are no permanent friends or permanent enemies, but only permanent interests. And our only permanent interest is profits . . . *our* profits." With that he turned to depart. He paused

---

[1] Truth always wins.

near the door for a final volley. "As for promises . . ." Dr G.O. Bells shrugged, "promises, my friend, are meant to be broken."

And that is exactly what he did the next day when he fired me. He did not give me the thirty-day notice that had been promised to me in my letter of appointment. He fired me for "salacious intent" and for being "a clear and present danger" to the organisation.

The minute they evicted me from The Promised Land I knew the Lord had shown me the way yet again. I knew my travails here in The Promised Land had not gone to waste, for as I was driving out of the gates, the wisdom of the Lord's Ninth Commandment flashed upon my inward eye and once again I felt my heart with pleasure fill, making me dance like a daffodil—

Thou Shalt always be Honest—in Thought, Word and Deed

The veracity of the Lords' wisdom was confirmed to me when I read in the papers a bit later that the Irate Guy had sued The Promised Land and the courts had decreed in his favour and granted him substantial damages while censuring The Promised Land for a whole load of things. To add to their misery the Municipal Corporation stopped a couple of their mega projects for not getting clearance from the Ministry of Environment.

Much as I did not wish to rejoice at the grief of others, I could not help but relish the picture of a crestfallen Dr G.O. Bells as he saw the hit on his bottom line. For once I thought this grief was well deserved. I just hoped they would all learn from this misfortune.

That is why I say unto you brother, "The nimble (of mind and tongue) may flourish for a while but they shall never inherit the earth."

- *It is better to under-commit and overachieve than to over-commit and under-achieve.*

- *Honesty of purpose is an inviolate prerequisite for success and must be maintained in thought, word and deed.*

- *Successful people are successful because people know that their word is their bond; so they trust them and will follow them.*

Thus spake Model . . .

Month Thirty-Three and Day Six P.D.A.

Thus spake Model . . .

I was still seething at the shoddy manner in which I had been treated at The Promised Land when I let myself into my apartment. Right on cue the phone began to ring. I didn't even have to hazard a guess as to who it was at the other end.

"Do you realise that I have never been so badly let down by a candidate in such a manner? No one placed by me has ever been fired for such behaviour." The Lord's headhunting lady accosted me coldly. "Do you have any idea how upset your wife is? In fact, I swear if she had not been my colleague I would not even have bothered to call you again . . . no matter how high your connections are." I am about to interrupt and plead my innocence, but she is in no mood to stop. "Even otherwise, let me assure you that this is positively the last time that I am ever going to place you anywhere. You mess this one up and you are so . . . so. . . ."

I am pretty sure that it was only her sheer professionalism and upbringing that prevented her from uttering the profanities that seemed to hover on the fringe of her tongue.

"Lady, will you listen to me . . ." I finally managed to get a word in edgewise. "I was framed . . . and I am sick of the depravity and cussedness of Man (and, to be honest, Woman also), especially towards their fellows." I can assure you that I would have gone on but that would have meant spilling the beans to her. My disillusionment was tempered only by the thought that I walked before God, my Lord. Also, I knew that having travelled so far I could not give up without completing the last of the ten labours assigned to me. "Oh forget it . . . it is a long story."

"Yeah, right!" She muttered disbelievingly. "Well, frankly I don't care. . . ."

"Whatever." I was really tired of it all and quite depressed at my inglorious eviction from The Promised Land. Maybe that is why her next words perked me up considerably.

"I have had a word with The Bank of Babel and Sodom. They will be happy to meet with you. Remember now . . . this is the last time, so don't mess it up," She added warningly.

"Oh, good! I always wanted to work there," I told her, thrilled to be back amongst the chosen ones.

"Well, you will if you get your interview right," she said. "Everything is almost finalised, you just have to meet Mr H. Adolph, the CEO of the Bank, at ten tomorrow. If you don't mess up that, you're in. Now be a little careful because he is a rather quirky guy."

"Quirky? In what way?"

"No one knows for sure, but he does weird things . . . like having his office in the basement three levels down. It is also said that he has this acute phobia about people bringing briefcases or laptop bags into his office."

We nattered on a bit more as she gave me more information about the bank and then we went our separate ways. The next day I realised what she had meant when I landed up at the bank.

"Step this way, sir . . . you need to walk through that." A huge security guard motioned towards the full-body metal detector spanning the door to Boss's office, when I reported for my interview.

Mr H. Adolph was sitting at the head of a huge square table when I entered. He waved a distant handshake at me and mumbled something. I didn't quite catch what he said, maybe because he had been fondling his moustache and the words must have gotten muffled behind his hand. At least that is what I thought at the time. It did not take me long to learn that disjointed mumbling was Mr H. Adolph's normal mode of communication. All of us at the Bank had to seriously strain our aural and mental senses to hear what he said and then try to figure out what he meant.

That day, during our first meeting.

"Let me begin by welcoming you to the Bank and telling you that you come most highly recommended by the consulting firm and we have great expectations from you. However," he wagged a finger at me, "your past performance would have no bearing on your future with the Bank. You need to keep up the good work if you want to bank on having a bright and prosperous future with the Bank."

I was a trifle hazed by it all, but (as is my policy when in the Boss's presence) I just flowed with the tide and yes-ed everything along.

Boss then mumbled something that sounded like, "We are feeling good to have you on board the Bank of Sodom and one day, if you work hard, deliver results and make us feel good, we may even feel good about having you on the board of the Bank of Sodom. The feel-good factor is very important. The Bank shall definitely make you feel good if you make us feel good. You can pretty much bank on it."

I replied with a polite "Thank you, sir."

He waved off my response with a vague gesture as he continued.

"Now, we are going to bank on you to ensure the Bank continues to feel good about banking on you. You must justify our feel-good feeling by working hard and making us feel even better by enhancing our market share and profitability."

"I can assure you that I will leave no stone unturned to ensure all this." I was about to go on but he mumbled on ahead of me.

"The feel-good factor is very critical." A longish pause. "Let me explain the Vision and Mission of the Bank." Another pause. "We want people to bank with us . . . lots of people . . . more than lots of people . . . the more the merrier . . . we will feel good about it . . . we want the Bank to have branches everywhere . . . *lots of branches* . . . the more the merrier . . . we will feel good about it. . . ."

He concluded these profound words with another vague dismissive gesture as he sent me off to toil and labour so that the Bank could continue to feel good.

It did not take me long to realise that if it had not been for the fact that Mr H. Adolph was surrounded by the most able and capable corporate generals, he would not have been able to translate any of his ideas into reality, as he was seldom able to communicate them to anyone in a meaningful manner.

Very shortly after I joined, we all received a formal e-mail from him. The mail went somewhat like this.

It pleases me to inform all of you that the Bank's performance over the last fiscal year gone by has been reviewed in detail by the Board based on the audit report submitted by the auditors and found to be generally okay but quite below projections. Now this, needless to state, is not a good state of affairs and not only does it not make us not feel good it will also adversely affect the monetary well-being and professional progress of all concerned.

Having stated this, let me also say that we all are not feeling good and are rather worried about this state of affairs and would like it to be reviewed and remedial action taken at all levels by all concerned. Keeping all this in view, I seriously think all of you should pull up your socks and let me have your clear and unequivocal views on how to make things better in this current fiscal year. We must have more and more and even more people in more and more villages, towns, cities and countries banking on us and with us. Many, many more people. I want all of you to think and act in a manner that makes me feel that the feel-good factor will be fully reinstated soon. If you make us feel good we will make all of you feel good. The feel-good factor is important.

The mail continued in the same vein for a few more paragraphs, but I was decidedly foggy by the time I had finished reading till here and my mind just shut down on me. However, so kicked was I at being back amongst the chosen ones that I did pull up my socks and got cracking.

As Director Sales (Small Credit and Finance) I knew just what was to be done. I called in my team.

"Guys, remember . . . smart thinking and relentless delegation. That is the key. I want you guys to launch a massive blitzkrieg."

"Don't worry, sir. Like Rommel romping all over Africa, we will be all over the place. We will ensure the other banks cower helplessly at the mere mention of our name," said one.

"We are going to spread the octopus-like tentacles of the Bank into the remote corners and interiors of the country," said another.

"Sir," said the third, "We are going to convince all small farmers and entrepreneurs to bank with us and take our loans."

Consequently, shortly thereafter our Bank spread like wildfire. You could not turn a corner even in the remote reaches of the country without being hit in the face by a board telling you The

Bank of Babel and Sodom awaited your pleasure. The results were astounding since the teeming multitudes came flocking to the Bank like rats following the Pied Piper.

However, soon thereafter, these very same farmers and entrepreneurs must have done something to invoke the fury of the Lord.

"Sir," one of my team members rushed in one day, "almost everyone who has taken loans from us has defaulted."

"Why?" I asked thoroughly dismayed.

"They are unable to pay us back because the plague of drought, famine, locusts, inflation, service tax, income tax and VAT has visited upon them."

I was not very happy to bear this news to Mr H. Adoph.

"Who gave them these loans?" he mumbled.

"Me and my team, sir," I replied manfully, stiffening my chin to face the inevitable.

"Did you give these against securities or were they unsecured?"

"Sir, they were secured . . . each and every one of them."

"Lovely!" He came around the table and shook my hand. "You have done well, my boy. I knew you had it in you. Now we can foreclosure on all of them and soon we will be the largest owner of land and businesses in the country."

Though it was the Director (Foreclosures and Recovery) who took direct action and foreclosed upon their lands and properties, I received great credits from Mr H. Adolph. Luckily I had taken great pains to ensure that my role in the aforesaid matter was duly highlighted and communicated to all and sundry at every possible moment. Some voice within had told me that it was as important to communicate one's achievements to the right quarters, as it was to accomplish them.

This whole thing found huge favour with Mr H. Adolph, as he was a firm believer in some concept called *Lebensraum*. He loved the idea of having laid his hands on so much real estate and so many business enterprises and went around telling everyone how good all this was making him feel.

"Now the sun is never going to be able to set on the Bank's empire." I heard him muttering once in a rare and unguarded moment. He went on to mumble something about someone called Rick or Reech, of dreams to be chased and legacies to be fulfilled. I am not too sure what he meant by all this and I found it all rather strange, but I was not very surprised since, like I told you, he was a rather quirky guy.

Anyway, he was really pleased with my performance and unique work style as I busily and assiduously went about implementing the Nine Commandments that the Lord had revealed to me so far. I'm sure they really helped in my growth and development because I seemed to be one of the happier and contented ones at the Bank.

Even though I was quite happy and the Bank had scaled great heights and was well on its way to glory, a nagging discontent gnawed at me because almost two years and two score days had passed since the Lord had visited me.

"Today is the last of the given days my Lord." I sent up a quick reminder prayer, just in case He had gotten busy and forgotten. "There is barely any time left for the sun to set and yet I cannot see hide nor hair of the Tenth Commandment."

To be honest what worried me greatly was the fact that this time the Lord had not been communicating the message to me loudly and clearly. Or maybe He was, but I was not getting the message properly. Anxious I was, but deep down I had implicit faith. I knew the Lord had not forsaken me. I knew the Lord would somehow communicate to me the wisdom of the Tenth before the deadline ran out.

Incidentally, it so happened that this day was an exceptionally auspicious one, in addition to being the stipulated divine deadline. The Bank was celebrating the Last Day of the Feast of Unleavened Profits. (These, as we all know, are different from the leavened profits that the Bank communicates to the taxman.)

"There shall be seven days of feasting this year," Mr H. Adolph had announced grandly. "This year the festivities must be huge since the Bank's turnover has more than doubled, great profits are in the offing and everyone must feel really good."

Consequently a huge repast flowed unchecked over the week.

"However," added the VP Finance, "with due respect for the economies of scale and the sensibilities of the shareholders, only three belly dancers had been flown in from Egypt." A groan went up from the gathered multitudes. He held up his hand for silence. When it returned he continued. "Please note that single malt servings will be restricted to four per head, peanuts will be served instead of cashew and aerated drinks instead of fruit juices to all below Senior Manager level." The groans became louder and a mite more threatening. "I'm just doing my job, folks." He protested mildly as he beat a hasty retreat.

As was the norm, at the beginning of the festivities the Book of Unleavened Profits had been handed over to Mr Anderson, the Director Finance. Over the week his army of highly creative chartered accountants had toiled relentlessly to ensure a smooth Passover of the Book from Unleavened to Leavened Profits.

Mr Anderson was a highly aggressive and warlike individual—quite like King Arthur. His assistant, Mr Young, though young in years, was a rather earnest soul and the perfect foil for his boss. They made a great team because they shared an uncanny rapport.

Through relentless toil, every year, they would ensure a smooth Passover of the books into another set that would then be handed over to Mr Pharaoh, our local taxman, so that he could levy taxes. Then, like good citizens, we would render unto Caesar what was rightfully his.

At the cessation of this Seventh day of feasting the Unleavened Books would be consigned to flames, so that no evidence of the Passover remained and the Leavened Books would be ceremoniously presented to Mr H. Adolph so that he may then pass them on (the next day) to Mr Pharaoh. At this same feast, Mr H. Adolph would also communicate the names of those who had excelled during this financial year and Annual Bonus for those who had toiled hard to push the Bank to greater glory.

"I am sure that great would be thy glory and huge thy bonus," said the Director HR to me as we sipped our single malts.

When the bells struck the Seventh Hour of the Seventh Day we all gathered around the fire for the final speeches. Ties were straightened and shirts and blouses tucked in properly as people converged towards the fire.

I, too, left the bar that I had been supporting so assiduously all evening and began walking towards the Director's Corner near the fire. That is where the table had been laid out for the Managing Director and the Top Twelve of the management team for the last supper, which was to be held after the Ceremony of the Flames.

I was halfway there when I was accosted by this rather severe-looking man in a badly cut black suit, who was accompanied by a trio of equally stern-looking men in black suits.

"What is happening here?" he asked of me.

I think it must have been the devil's brew that had affected my senses so badly, else I would surely have questioned him more closely afore I communicated any meaningful information to him.

However, as things turned out, I threw my innate caution to the winds and said to him, "We are all gathering around the fire for the Passover."

"The Passover?" he queried, a mite more gently this time. "What is that all about?"

"That is when the Book of Leavened Profits is handed over to Mr H. Adolph so that he may hand it over to Mr Pharaoh on the morrow and the Book of Unleavened Profits is consigned to the flames so that it may carry its secret to the grave."

"What, pray, is the Book of Unleavened Profits?" he asked.

I laughed heartily, for surely no man could be so naïve and lacking in common business knowledge. He must be new to the corporate battlefield or, at the very least, mentally challenged not to know all this. Surely it was my duty to enhance his knowledge levels and save his soul by communicating the truth to him.

"Surely you jest, thou kindly knave!" I guffawed. "The Book of Unleavened Profits is a record of what we have actually earned in this fiscal year. When the Accounts Army has gone over this book and added creative touches to it, then it passes over into the Book of Leavened Profits, which shows only what we want to show as profits to Mr Pharaoh, our local Taxman."

"Really?" The severe-looking man looked at me strangely as he too guffawed a bit. "Is that what happens at the Passover?"

"But of course, my dear man. Come, come let me show you . . . the Ceremony of the Flames is about to begin . . ." I said to him, taking his arm and tugging him closer to the fire. The trio with him followed closely behind.

"Look!" I said, pointing towards Mr Anderson the Director Accounts as he walked up to the fire carrying two data disks held up high in the air. "There they are! The two books. Now watch closely as Mr H. Adolph, after the final prayer and toast, consigns the Book of Unleavened Profits to the Holy Fire."

We all watched. The prayer was about to begin. We could see the piano player strike a few tentative chords, the choir take final sips of water and the belly dancers give small warming up twirls to their bellies.

"But who art thou and how is it that thou knowest not these simple facts of life?"

"Me?" said the severe-looking man, a strange light in his eyes. I felt a million spiders crawl up my spine at the evil sneer that smeared across his face. "I am Pharaoh."

His words struck home like fists of fury. Like Lot's wife I stood frozen, for I had the sudden sinking feeling that I should have thought over things more carefully before I communicated with a stranger. Pharaoh turned to the unholy trio behind him.

"Seize those men!" He bellowed, pointing at Mr Anderson and Mr H. Adolph. "And those disks." He reached inside his coat and pulled out a walkie-talkie. "Ghazi Two!" He screamed into the walkie-talkie. "Ghazi Two! Now! *Now*! *NOW*!"

Within seconds a horde of (ill-suited and robust-looking) young men in black stormed out of the shadows and swarmed over the area like hungry locusts on a new field. Immediately I saw Mr H. Adolph and Mr Anderson leaning against the wall, their legs apart and hands held high in the air as Pharaoh's men surrounded them with drawn guns. Pharaoh walked up to them with a sadistic smile playing on his thin, mean lips.

"Mr Adolph. I cannot tell you what a pleasure this is."

He patted him paternally on his shoulder as he spoke. Then, turning towards Anderson, retrieved the two disks from his upraised hands.

"*Mister* Anderson, you have a problem with authority."

I looked at my watch and saw that barely three minutes remained before the two years and two score days stipulated by the Lord ran out. Right then I knew, without doubt, what the Lord had wished to communicate to me. In a flash the words of the Tenth Commandment were upon me—

Thou Shalt always Communicate Clearly, Concisely and only when Required

The words of the Lord ran through my mind again and again as I saw Mr H. Adolph and Mr Anderson being led away by Pharaoh's men. They ran through my mind as I saw his evil army cart away tons of documents and cartons of data disks. They ran through my mind as I was grilled and questioned for hours by Pharaoh's interrogators. They were still running through my mind as I finally staggered home the next day, drained and exhausted beyond words.

I was busy cursing the stars that had unleashed such misery on me, when I realised that I was amongst the luckier ones. Mr H. Adolph and Mr Anderson were released from jail on bail only three days later. I was there at the offices when they returned. They looked morose and sombre. I felt an inner compulsion to try and cheer them up.

"Hullo, Boss . . . how are you . . . hi Mr Anderson . . . my, but you two are looking really lean, mean and physically so fit. I think the prison diet and regimen must have suited you."

"Huh!" They both gave me long, meaningful looks. I was amazed to note that they did not seem to appreciate my compliment

one whit. Then they looked at each other and grunted—harshly.
As they walked away I got the feeling that for some strange reason
they seemed to blame me for the whole thing.

Shortly thereafter the office messenger came up to me and
handed over a small shoebox-sized carton. Upon opening the carton
I spied a small envelope. Below that was a medium-sized leather
pouch tied with a thong. Opening the envelope, I came across a
terse letter written to me.

*Sir, This is to inform you that the post held by you at the Bank has
been made redundant, hence your services are no longer required, and as far
as the Bank is concerned we are damn certain they are never ever going to be
required again. You can bank on that. The cheque for salary in lieu of notice
period is enclosed. The annual bonus is in the leather pouch. Goodbye.
Dr H. Adolph.*

I felt an immediate sense of relief for this meant that the Tenth
and Final Commandment lay within my grasp. Before I got down
to looking for it, I decided to put more mundane matters to rest.
I scrutinised the cheque. It was for the correct amount and correctly
made out.

The leather pouch yielded thirty pieces of silver. I found this
rather inexplicable. This was the first time in my life that I had
heard of anyone paying the annual bonus with thirty pieces of silver.
I felt cheated too, for I knew beyond doubt that my annual bonus
should have been far more than the thirty pieces of silver that had
been thrown at me so uncouthly. But by now I had become used
to being persecuted by my fellow humans as I walked in the path
of God, my Lord. However, knowing that they did not know what
they were doing, I promptly forgave them and deposited the thirty
pieces of silver in my bank locker.

In any case I had the consolation of knowing that the wisdom of the Tenth Commandment was worth more than all the silver in Fort Knox.

- *The human tongue can wreak untold havoc if wielded unwisely.*

- *Information is of value only if it is swiftly and clearly communicated.*

- *Brilliance and genius are of no practical value unless one is able to communicate one's thoughts and ideas to others, because only then does an idea translate into reality.*

- *Communication is a critical leadership trait that can be developed with regular practice.*

- *Successful people are successful because they are able to communicate their thoughts clearly and do not speak without due forethought.*

Thus spake Model . . .

Chapter 9

May the Force be With You

Thus spake Model . . . and having spoken thus, he finally stopped speaking.

By now the moon was well on its way to waning. A new dawn was about to break. To me, in some mysterious way, it symbolised the dawn of a new era—a new beginning that promised more happiness, fulfilment and contentment for the entire human race.

At about the beginning of the witching hour we had left the Guitar Club where Model had begun his story and walked across to the gardens around India Gate. There we had sat, bathed by the tranquil moonlight as Model had spoken and I, his faithful scribe, had recorded his words for posterity on my trusted Dictaphone.

Undisturbed we had been, but for the occasional passing cop who wanted to know what we were doing there at this time of the night, or that occasional potential mugger who contemplated the potentially lucrative target that we offered. However by and large they all left us alone.

The bottle of Holy Spirit we had carried with us had long been extinguished. Yet it bothered us not one whit since even the water we carried tasted just as wholesome and refreshing once Model had but touched his hand to the bottle.

For a very long time after he finished we sat in total silence. I was totally overcome by the sheer magnitude of all that had been revealed to me. I was also deeply shaken by the suffering that Model had endured in his pursuit of the Divine Truth.

However, beyond everything, the sheer beauty of the wisdom that had been passed on to me overwhelmed me. I rejoiced that I had been chosen to deliver it to mankind; yet, at the same time I was plagued by my ability to deliver the goods.

Finally Model spoke. "Hast thou gotten everything that thou needs to deliver unto Mankind the wisdom of the Lord?"

"Yea. Yea, I do, Master," I replied, patting my Dictaphone. "But are you sure you want me to write about it? Suppose they do not believe me or listen to me, but say, 'The Lord did not appear to Model.'"

Model looked at me unperturbed and replied, "See the pen in thy hands. Strike it down on the ground in front of them and tell them, 'See the wisdom that flows out of it.' If they still do not believe thee, press rewind and replay thy Dictaphone. With these signs they shall surely believe."

"Will these signs be enough, my brother? Will I be able to convince them? You know I'm a shy and diffident kind of guy. What if they heckle me into silence?"

"Then warn them that they must not forsake and anger the Lord, lest He unleashes upon them the Ten Plagues and condemns them to the dungeons of mediocrity."

"Okie dokie Master. If you say so."

"Don't worry too much about it, my boy. The Lord shall show you the way as he did me. Have faith in Him and put your mind to rest. Now, just tell me if there is anything else that you wish to know or do you have all that you need to deliver the Lord's word to all mankind?"

"Yea brother, fret thee not. I do, and I shall deliver to Man the message in thy very own words, for I detect the words of the Lord in them."

"Amen."

"Hallelujah."

"Go forth then, my brother. Do thy duty without fear, for the Lord is thy shepherd and nothing shall stand in thy way."

A long pause as Model seemed to be searching for the right words to set me off on The Path. Then with a clenched fist high in the air, his voice boomed out and echoed decisively through the fog that floated in the early morning air.

"May the Force be with you!"

Thus it came to pass . . .

Chapter 10

Thus It Came to Pass… that these Words Come Unto You

It took me well-nigh seven moons to put down on paper the entire story that Model had told me. Countless were the nights that I sat up with the stars thumping on the keys of my laptop. That night when I finally finished the priceless tale, I slept with a much lighter heart knowing that I had done the duty the Lord had bidden me and quite eagerly looked forward to calling Model with the good news.

The next morning, the minute the rays of the new sun ushered in the new day, I called Model. He greeted me most effusively.

"Peace, brother. 'Tis glad that I am to hear from thee. Hast thou made any progress with the Lord's work?"

"Shalom, Master," I replied with an unseemly pride flowing through my voice. "By the grace of the Lord and, of course, thy blessings, I am well. And I have done the work that you commanded me to do. In fact, that is the reason I have called thee this glorious morn."

"Good man!" I could tell he was pleased at my diligence. "God bless you! Then bring me the manuscript, brother."

"Yea, Master, I will since I too really wish to meet you again."

"Good, good. So be it. Come to the Lodi Garden tomorrow at the crack of dawn. I shall meet you there."

"Right, Master. Whereabouts in the garden shall I find thee?"

"The Lord shall show you the way." Then Model put down the phone.

When I reached Lodi Garden the next morning it took me just a fraction of a second to spot Model. There he was, across the angry and glimmering waters of the little pool in the middle of the garden, perched on a mound of freshly dug mud, just a little away from the savage fury of the hedge running all along the garden. The rays of the rising sun settled upon him like a divine halo, adding to the grace of the staid gray pin-striped suit that clothed his person. I just walked up to him and wordlessly laid the manuscript at his feet. He made the holy sign of approval and silently blessed me.

"Before I go through the manuscript, my brother, let me tell you that I am extremely proud of you. I am happy that you have dedicated yourself so selflessly to the Lord's work. I shall definitely commend you to the Lord when I meet him again."

I was, of course, thrilled with this praise and the fact that I was going to be commended to the top man Himself. "Thank you, Master. I thank you most kindly. When are you meeting the Lord again?"

"Soon I am sure." Model replied with a world of conviction in his tone. "He will call me when the time is right."

"Master, can you take me with you when you go to seek the Lord?" I asked him quite eagerly.

Model gave it a moment's thought and then shook his head gravely.

"No, my son, that I cannot do since I have not checked with the Lord and don't know how He will react to an unsolicited audience, but I shall come back and tell you in detail what the Lord had to say."

"Okay, Master, it shall be as you say." I was rather disappointed but I could quite see his point of view. "I guess it would be rather rude to barge in on the Lord unannounced and uninvited."

He nodded. A short silence reigned thereafter.

Then Model picked up the manuscript and began to read it. The rest of the day passed in wordless silence as he read and I sat at his lotus feet awaiting his judgement with bated breath. Barring an hour or so for a quick beer and a spot of lunch, Model did not give himself even a moment's respite.

The sun was about to extinguish the light of yet another day when he finally turned the last page. He shut the book and held it in his hands for a long time before he finally put it down (rather reverently, I might add) and then looked up at me. I thought there was a hint of tears sparkling in his eyes. There definitely was a catch in his voice as he spoke.

"Son, you have done a great job. I am deeply touched and moved beyond words."

I felt my chest swell at such unprecedented praise from one so exalted. My voice trembled as I thanked him profusely.

"Thank you, Master, thank you so much. I was but the humble scribe who merely transferred your words to paper."

"No, no," Model shook his head gravely, "you are too modest. You are a wordsmith worthy of great renown. In fact, I think you are not aptly named. You should have been called Shakespen."

"You mean Shakespeare, Master?" I corrected gently.

"No, I mean Shakespen, for the pen is mightier than the spear."

There was yet another brief pause while we both collected our thoughts. Then he spoke again.

"Right then, brother. Now take this divine manuscript to the biggest and best publisher on the planet. Tell him to spread the Lord's word to each and every corner of the world without further ado or delay."

He kissed the manuscript reverently and handed it back to me.

"I shall call you when I return from my meeting with the Lord."

Then Model gave me a Go-with-God wave and he was gone.

THEREFORE I SAY UNTO YOU

Friends, countrymen and all ye struggling peoples
To prosper and find peace seek not demons or angels

Instead lend me thy ears I thee beseech
Open thy mind and hearken unto my speech

For I come not to take in vain the name of the Lord
I have come to spread His Word

And the Word is

Should ye wish to prosper and find peace and happiness
Then seek precious wisdom that is timeless and priceless

Beware of False Prophets and always remember
If ye work smart and not just hard ye shall surely prosper

Be a true and faithful servant and follow to the T
These Ten Commandments the Lord has given thee

Lest the ten plaques like Heaven's knives
Alight on thee and blight thy lives

AMEN

Chapter 11

For Whosoever Drinketh of this Water Shall Never Thirst Again

The time has come dear reader, for me to pass on and leave thee with The Word. Read. Ponder. Mull. Understand. And, I beseech thee to forsake not the Lord and to follow these Ten Commandments faithfully.

Remember, Dear Reader, Thou must always:

1. TAKE NOTES AND BE ORGANISED

2. DRESS SMARTLY AND EXUDE A POSITIVE ATTITUDE

3. REMAIN FIRMLY FOCUSED ON THE SELECTED AIM

4. SEEK OUT THE BEST IN PEOPLE AND HELP THEM LIVE UP TO THEIR POTENTIAL

5. NOT WORRY ABOUT THINGS THAT YE CANNOT CONTROL

6. RESPECT TIME—YOURS AND THAT OF OTHERS

7. TAKE CARE OF THY HEALTH SO THOU CAN LIVE A FRUITFUL LIFE

8. KEEP THY PERSONAL AND PROFESSIONAL LIVES APART

9. BE HONEST—IN THOUGHT, WORD AND DEED

10. COMMUNICATE CLEARLY, CONCISELY AND ONLY WHEN REQUIRED

These simple steps shall enable you to live a long, successful and happy life.

With this, I thee leave. But before I go, I must also tell you, it is important you understand that there may be some of you, who *despite your best efforts*, may fail to understand or implement faithfully these invaluable Ten Commandments that M.O.D.E.L. has passed on to us as a divine legacy. For these unfortunate few, to help you complete the journey of life as successfully as possible, let me pass on this omnipotent and omniscient nugget of wisdom:

IF AT FIRST YOU DON'T SUCCEED,

DON'T SWEAT IT

BECOME A CONSULTANT

~ The gospel according to M.O.D.E.L.

Now dear reader, 'tis time for me to bring to an end this enthralling saga of 'M.O.D.E.L.—The Model Employee'. This, however, by no means implies that this is the end of the M.O.D.E.L. saga.

Model like Methuselah shall live for at least 969 years. He is an evergreen life form that we humans shall never see the end of. His story is like Existence itself; it has no beginning and no end. Like the circle of Life it goes on and on.

Not very far in the future, I shall come back to you with yet another episode of the M.O.D.E.L. saga that will bring much wanted relief to those hundreds of beleaguered Employers. They, too, constitute humanity and must not be allowed to perish, for they are a part of the circle of Life. As the deer is to the lion, the fly is to the lizard and the frog is to the snake, even so is the employee to the employer. They both need each other, feed and thrive off each other. With all his infinite wisdom, Model shall soon return to bring them the much-needed relief, in—

M.O.D.E.L.—The Employer Strikes Back!

About the Author

Mukul Deva studied at La Martiniere College, Lucknow; the National Defence Academy, Pune; and the Indian Military Academy, Dehra Dun. Commissioned in the Sikh Light Infantry of the Indian Army, he took premature retirement as a Major after fifteen years of service. Mukul Deva is now an entrepreneur operating out of Delhi. He is the Managing Director of MSD Security Private Limited and Founding Director of CAN*assist*.

His published titles include *Time After Time...It All Happened* and *S.T.R.I.P.T.E.A.S.E.— The Art of Corporate Warfare*.